HOW CAN I STOP WORRYING?

The definitive 5-step process to help you smooth away your worries

KAY JOHNSON

First published in 2020 by Waterleaf Publishing Ltd

ISBN: 978-1-5272-5816-7

Disclaimer

The ideas and opinions expressed in this book are those of the author who is acting in good faith following her application of many different stress management techniques over a long period of time. The author confirms that she uses the techniques included here to overcome the worries associated with everyday living.

This book is intended to provide information about how to deal with doubts, worries and concerns, and is sold on the understanding that the author and publisher are not engaged in providing medical or other professional services. While every effort has been made to ensure the accuracy of the information provided here, the author and publisher do not accept responsibility for any liability, loss, injury or damages, whether direct or indirect, as a result of using and applying the contents of this book.

The techniques outlined in this book may not be suitable for everyone, and are not guaranteed or warranted to produce any particular results.

If you suffer from, or are likely to be suffering from, any form of anxiety disorder, or have experienced abuse or trauma, you must consult a qualified medical professional before using any of the techniques outlined in this book. And if, after starting to use these techniques, you develop any signs or symptoms you didn't have before, you must also discuss these with a qualified medical professional to make sure it's safe to continue.

Acknowledgements

This book is the result of a journey over the last 25 years, during which I have changed the way I view life's difficulties, and how I deal with the troubles and worries we all face at one time or another. I have learnt a lot from many different gurus, but would particularly like to mention six people who have helped transform my life for the better.

First, I extend my thanks to the great motivational speakers, Brian Tracy and Zig Ziglar, for helping me appreciate the power of thought. This was the first step in learning how to deal with my doubts and concerns more effectively. Next, I would like to mention Bob Proctor and Bill Harris who helped improve my understanding of why we don't always get what we want in life. And finally, my thanks go to David R Hamilton and Joe Dispenza for explaining the link between the mind and the body, and how our thoughts are feelings are interrelated.

I also would not have learnt how to manage stress and worry in practice had it not been for the many challenges that life provided. Without these opportunities, I would never have honed my worry management skills, nor built the confidence to tackle and come through various health, family and work-related problems.

And last, but by no means least, I would like to thank my family and friends for their enormous support over the years, and in particular for their belief in me, and being there, no matter what.

Contents

WELCOME

WELCOME

I am delighted to bring you this book which is the result of many years of work exploring how best to overcome the doubts and worries we all face in life.

No matter how angst-ridden you're feeling, you really can get lasting relief from all your concerns, and find some peace of mind. You don't need any special skills or qualities, and you don't need any special training; you just need to know what to do, and then apply it in your everyday life, which is where the *How Can I Stop Worrying?* step-by-step process comes in. It's a straightforward 5-step process that will help transform your life for the better.

MY STORY

Go back over 25 years and ever since I could remember, I had worried about everything that came my way, wondering if I could cope. What if I didn't find the man of my life? What if I couldn't work? What if I didn't have enough money to pay the bills? What if I had a life-threatening illness? What if I made a fool of myself? And so on.

I was overwhelmed at work and could barely keep my head above water. I had research studies to conduct, staff to manage, client meetings to attend and public speaking commitments to fulfil. I just couldn't come up for air. What's more, I often found myself working with people who had very different values and priorities to my own.

On the brighter side, my family and social life was brimming over. I had great holidays, played lots of sport, went to films and concerts, took up new hobbies and enjoyed catching up with friends and relatives. But looking back, I realise I never stopped.

Worst of all, two personal relationships ran their course and finished with all the emotional turmoil that parting brings. I was heartbroken. My world turned upside down.

Then came the wake-up call…

Even though I was a born worrier, I kept going – no matter what – until that awful moment when I felt like I was going around in a bubble, disconnected from the rest of the world. I could see out, but felt so isolated from everything going on around me. Struggling to cope, my body just gave up. I'd had a few minor health problems before, but nothing quite like this. I was so weak and exhausted, I was sleeping 16 hours a day, had all sorts of digestive problems and lost a huge amount of weight. Turns out my immune system was shot to bits and it took 18 months to get my health back on track.

I knew I needed help restoring my physical strength and stamina, but it also dawned on me that if I wanted to find some peace of mind and lasting happiness, something had to change inside my head. My old ways of dealing with life's ups and downs just weren't working.

And that was the turning point…

I started reading books and articles, visiting websites and listening to recorded seminars about how to deal with stress and worry. I consulted literally hundreds of different sources over the next few years, and through trial and error, gradually found out what worked and what didn't. I came to realise that there are five steps we can take to relieve our doubts and concerns. These are the steps I would like to share with you in this book.

As I started to apply them in my everyday life, I noticed that, little by little, problems seemed easier to sort out. Things that would have sent my stress level soaring became more manageable. And demanding people weren't so difficult to deal with. Things started looking up. Best of all, situations that would have filled me with fear lost their hold on me. They became challenges to overcome and move on. I found I could handle things I previously thought were impossible, and each time this happened, my confidence and self-esteem went up a notch. I was over the moon!

Since going on this life-changing journey, my 5-step approach has been put to the test many times, often in heart-rending situations. I've since used it to overcome the anguish associated with financial worries, relationship break-ups, illness, caring for family members, demanding work situations, constant deadlines, dealing with difficult people, public speaking and business set-up. I'm now blessed with good health, happiness and peace of mind, and enjoy life to the full. Yes, problems still come my way, but I'm no longer tortured by agonising worry.

So, if you're weighed down by doubts and concerns, I suggest trying the approach outlined in this book. It's not the only way of dealing with worry, but it has worked for me time and again.

WHY I WROTE THIS BOOK

When I hit on the idea of writing this book, it was, first and foremost, to share with as many people as possible the steps that have helped me overcome stress and worry. If they could help me – a former 5-star worrier, who would have graduated with honours had there been a qualification in worrying – they could help others.

Secondly, so much of the material I read when I was going through my learning phase was very difficult to absorb. There were undoubtedly profound concepts and ideas, but it often took days of reading to understand them fully and distil them into helpful bite-size chunks.

And finally, at the other end of the spectrum, some of the material seemed very simplistic. In my experience, it's no good saying: *all you have to do is x, y and z, and instantly, your worries will become a thing of the past.* It's not quite that straightforward. Worries don't suddenly evaporate. But here's the thing: immobilising worries can become a thing of the past by applying a few straightforward steps on an ongoing basis. It just takes a bit of time and practice.

RESTORE YOUR INNER PEACE AND REVIVE YOUR ZEST FOR LIFE

One of the problems many of us face is that we have been conditioned into thinking we have to accept doubt and worry as part of our life, because there's no other option. That's just the way we are. But I discovered that's not the case. The 5-step process outlined in this book provides a framework you can use on a daily basis to find some inner calm and restore your peace of mind.

It will enable you to remove that sense of oppression caused by constant doubt and worry. It will stop worry from taking a toll on your mental, physical and emotional well-being. It will increase your confidence and self-belief. It will put you in control again. It will restore a sense of calm deep inside. And it will allow you to reignite your love of life and all you enjoy doing.

And the great thing about it is that you can use it anytime and anywhere.

There isn't going to be an overnight transformation. This is not a quick fix. And if I were to suggest this were the case, quite rightly, with your experience of worrying, you wouldn't believe me. But what I can say is that it's eminently possible to restore your inner peace and revive your zest for life by applying the 5-step process consistently on a day-by-day basis.

A happier life really does await you.

SUGGESTED APPROACH

The book is divided into three parts.

Part 1 (Chapters 1–2) provides an introduction to worry and, in particular, explores the myths which surround it. It's worth reading these two chapters, because they put worry into context, and explain why it's possible to move on from a life dominated by doubts and fears.

Part 2 (Chapters 3-5) covers what I call the key to success. It involves unlocking the mystery of the mind, before outlining the 5-step process for dealing with the worries in your life. Now you may be tempted to skip Chapters 3 and 4, but I suggest taking time to go through them, because they explain the theory on which the 5-step process is based. Then you will come to Chapter 5, which is essential reading and where you will discover the steps you can take to help smooth away your worries.

Part 3 (Chapters 6-10) expands on the 5-step process. At this point, you may choose to focus on certain chapters and skip others. That is your choice.

Chapter 6 covers letting go of the past, because so much of what we all worry about is tied up with what's gone before in our lives. Chapters 7 and 8 outline how to put an end to blame and resentment, as well as how to overcome guilt, shame and regret. These issues can be deeply troubling and self-destructive if they're allowed to take hold, so you need a technique that enables you to let go of them once and for all.

Chapter 9 explores how to overcome self-doubt and build an inner confidence that allows you to deal more effectively with the difficulties you're facing in life.

And finally, Chapter 10 details some of the most common mistakes that are made when trying to stop worry, as well as suggested next steps.

At the end of every chapter, you will find a summary of the key points covered, so if you need to refresh your memory about the content, you can go straight to that part of the text. Importantly, the key points include tips that will help you apply what's been discussed in your own life. Many of the chapters also conclude with a series of questions you can ask yourself to help fine tune the steps you can take to deal with particular worries.

The aim of this book is to give you a set of tools that you can use to overcome your troubles and worries. Throughout the text, there are examples of how to deal with particular types of worry, whether they be money troubles, demanding work situations, relationship problems, dealing with difficult people or health concerns.

Should you require any further information, you can go to my website: https://www.soothingyoursoul.com

THE PATH TO GREATER HAPPINESS

It is my deeply held wish that the 5-step process outlined in this book will enable you to overcome the doubts and worries you may be experiencing.

Even if you're someone who has worried all your life, it really is possible to change and find some peace of mind. With a little bit of time and practice, the 5-step process will unlock the door to greater happiness, where you feel in control on the inside, no matter what's happening on the outside. And most importantly, it will allow you to achieve a life where you feel calm, confident and relaxed; a life where you enjoy your work and leisure, and where you spend quality time with your family and friends.

If this born worrier can change, I believe you can too.

To your health and happiness,

Kay Johnson

PART 1:
INTRODUCTION

CHAPTER 1: WHAT IS WORRY?

WHERE TO START

The starting point in learning how to stop worrying is to take a look at exactly what worry is, why some people worry more than others, and why it's possible to change.

You might ask why do we need to dig down and take a detailed look at worry? We all know what it's like to feel angst-ridden and stressed out of our minds. We just want to get rid of it, so why not skip straight to the 5-step process?

It's a good question.

Yes, we all know what worry feels like, but until you understand how worry is actually created and what causes it to persist, you can't be effective in smoothing it out of your life and finding some peace of mind.

Prior to learning how all this worked, I'd tried for years 'not to worry'. But every time I tried 'not to worry', I found myself worrying even more. It was a bit like someone saying to me: *you can think about anything except a green elephant*, and all I could think about was a green elephant.

Go back 25 years and I was constantly worried about what might go wrong. How was I going to sort out a problem I didn't know how to solve? What if I made a really bad mistake? What if I lost my job? What if my long-term relationship fell apart? And on and on. I was really feeling the strain.

I thought my tendency to worry was just how it was, and that there was nothing I could do about it. I labelled myself a born worrier and that was that.

But I was wrong; there was something I could do about it.

After I went down with a crash, I started exploring how best to deal with stress and worry. And what I discovered is that there have been huge scientific advances in understanding the power of the mind, and in particular, how it can be harnessed to help us overcome the difficulties we face in life. I tried all sorts of different techniques, and little by little, found out how to subdue my doubts and fears, and restore my inner calm. Things that would have sent my stress level soaring became more manageable. And demanding people weren't so difficult to deal with.

The lesson I've learnt along the way is that we really can tame our doubts and fears, and restore our peace of mind...no matter what's happening in our lives. And how to do it is what I would like to share with you in this book.

But first it's important to understand a bit more about worry itself.

WHAT IS WORRY?

Worry is part of everyday living. It comes as part and parcel of being human, and although it's often not very pleasant, it's an essential aspect that's been hard-wired into all of us to help us survive and cope with the difficulties we all face in life.

You can think of it as **any negative thoughts or feelings that happen inside in response to an actual or potential problem that we're facing**.

The reason we worry about something is because we see it as a threat to our well-being, so we focus on it in an attempt to protect ourselves. And indeed, there are some very real dangers in everyday life – dangers to our health, security and happiness – that we need to be aware of so we can find answers to these problems and take reasonable steps to protect ourselves from harm.

So, worry has its good points.

THE PROBLEM WITH WORRY

But worry can become a major issue if this realistic type of concern morphs into a preoccupation that goes way beyond a reasonable interest in protecting ourselves and finding an answer to our problems.

Not only can it detract from the pleasures in life and make us feel miserable, it can also be very destructive, particularly if it becomes so absorbing that we can't think about anything else. It can interfere with our ability to connect with other people, it can stop us from fulfilling our family, work and personal responsibilities, and can even immobilise us completely so we simply can't do what we need to do.

The challenge for all of us is how to stop our worries from running riot in our minds and undermining all the good things in our lives, especially our happiness, well-being and peace of mind. And the good news is that this is eminently possible for *everyone*, even if you're a constant worrier.

WORRY IS VERY PERSONAL

One of the things that's important to remember, whether you're dealing with your own worries, or the worries of someone close to you, is that worry is very personal. What one person worries about, someone else may see as a challenge, a source of excitement or even 'no big deal'. But just because someone else isn't bothered by something that's causing you great angst doesn't mean it's not real to you. In fact, it can be all absorbing.

As an aside, you sometimes hear people drawing the distinction between so-called 'real' and 'imaginary' worries, which I don't think is helpful. I believe there is a distinction between 'actual' and 'potential' worries (i.e. between something you're facing right now and something that might happen in the future), but if you're worried about something, whatever it is, to you, it's a very real worry. So please don't take any notice if other people say your concerns are 'imaginary'.

What's more, keep in mind there's nothing wrong with you because you're worried about something and nobody else is. We all worry at some time or another, it's just that we worry about different things. The 5-step process is designed to help get rid of your worries, whatever they may be and no matter what others may think about your concerns.

WHY SOME PEOPLE WORRY MORE THAN OTHERS

There are four things that influence the extent to which you worry.

- The first is your genetic make-up, or hard wiring, which shapes your personality from the moment you're born. Some people, through no fault of their own, are predisposed to worrying; they always see what might go wrong and constantly focus on that.
- The second influence is your upbringing and what happens in your formative years. If those close to you viewed the world as a threatening place and were anxious about what they had to deal with in everyday life, you may have learnt to respond in the same way.

- Then there are the experiences you've gone through. If something upsetting happened to you in the past that you weren't able to come to terms with at the time, you may feel stressed about facing the same sort of situation again in the future.
- And last, but by no means least, is your ability to learn new ways of dealing with worrying situations. **And this is good news for all worriers**, because irrespective of your personality, upbringing and past experiences, it's possible to learn how to deal with stress and worry more effectively.

THE LINK WITH STRESS

When you're worried about something, it's because your mind and body have been subjected to something stressful, typically triggered by:

- The external demands of life, or
- Your internal thoughts and feelings, and any physical demands on your body

When thinking about the external demands of life, there are literally hundreds – maybe even thousands – of possible triggers, including dealing with difficult people, divorce, being in crowded places, the pressure of work, deadlines, public speaking, explaining a mistake, moving house or any other type of change.

Similarly, there are countless internal triggers, such as concerns about the future, what might go wrong or a fear of messing up, as well as feelings of guilt, regret, a crisis of confidence or perceptions about such things as whether you think you're a good parent or hard-working employee. And finally, there are physiological triggers such as pain, illness and sleeping problems.

What actually happens is that worry kicks in when you're concerned about whether you can cope with a threat you're facing or the demands being made on you. And just to emphasise, you're not alone. Everyone experiences stress and worry.

But the harsh reality is that all of the triggers mentioned here are part of everyday life; you can't avoid them. The key is learning how to manage them, so they don't undermine your physical and emotional well-being.

STRESS ISN'T NECESSARILY BAD

When you're beside yourself with worry, it's almost impossible to imagine that there could be anything good about stress. You just want to get rid of it, and get rid of it fast. But the truth of the matter is that **some** pressure is actually good for us all. The trick is to stay on the motivational – or even exciting – side of the line rather than flip over onto the stress-filled side.

If you think about what has given you the greatest satisfaction in life, it was probably something you had to work really hard at, something that was a real challenge or which involved learning a new skill. Although it was demanding and you felt under pressure, you got a real buzz from what you accomplished. For that reason, what you experienced can be thought of as **good** stress.

In contrast, there are those situations where you're under so much pressure you feel trapped, unable to walk away; it's as though something's being done to you. This is **bad** stress and the sort we all hate, because it can undermine your well-being if it's not managed effectively.

So, what can we learn from all this? The key lies in…

TAPPING INTO THE CHARACTERISTICS OF GOOD STRESS

There are three characteristics that differentiate good stress from bad stress:

- The first is that you have some degree of **control** over the stressful situation.
- The second is you can **choose** if you're going to participate in the stressful situation and, if so, how you intend to deal with it.
- And finally, good stress has a **purpose**. It may be the achievement of something you've set your heart on or a challenge you're determined to overcome; either way, the stress you experience is in order to achieve a desired outcome.

So, you can see that good stress is a great motivator that inspires you to strive for wonderful things and lead a more fulfilling life. Learning a new skill can be stressful, but the pleasure and opportunities that follow can be enormous. Standing up to a difficult boss, friend or family member can test your nerve, but it heightens your self-esteem. Public speaking can be petrifying, but it boosts your self-confidence.

In contrast, bad stress is a great demotivator. If you've been laid off, have a serious illness, or your partner has walked out, it's difficult to find anything that's good about these situations. You certainly would not have chosen any of them and, on the face of it, you have little control over them. But, there's light at the end of the tunnel, because the characteristics of good stress – control, choice and purpose – can be **applied** to situations involving bad stress.

CHANGING YOUR RESPONSE TO STRESS

When you're angst-ridden and consumed with worry, the harmful effects actually come from your **response** to the stressful situation, **not** the stressful situation itself. It can be very difficult to accept this when you're confronting all sorts of difficulties in your life.

But, by changing the way you respond to the problems you're facing, you can transform bad stress – and the associated worry – into something more manageable. And most importantly, you can find relief in even the most dire of situations. This isn't a superficial, quick fix recommendation that will fall apart tomorrow; this is a life-changing transformation that really can bring about some peace of mind.

Sadly, you can't change the situation if you need major surgery, if your company has gone into receivership or if you're faced with the heart-breaking reality that your partner has left you for someone else. These are events beyond your control, but **what you can change is your response to the situation**.

You may say: *I don't deserve what's happening to me,* which may well be true. You may think: *I'll never find another job,* but that's a false impression. Or you may shout: *it's all his fault,* but blame won't solve the problem.

The reality is that these understandable responses only exacerbate worry and send your stress level through the ceiling. You won't find relief while you're consumed with anxiety or other destructive thoughts, because these negative emotions only immobilise you. You can't change other people – only they can do that – and you often can't change the circumstances in which you find yourself, but you can change how you deal with the situation.

And if you find yourself thinking: *why should I be the one to change?* The answer is quite simple: you need to change in the interests of restoring your peace of mind, enhancing your well-being and improving the quality of your life.

TAKING CONTROL OF YOUR LIFE AGAIN

When you're worried out of your mind, it's very easy to get locked into the idea that you've got no choice and have to accept whatever's happening to you, but this isn't the case, it's only how things **seem**.

The key to dealing with your worries is recognising that you **have a choice about how you respond by changing the things over which you have complete control**, namely:

- The way you think about your problems.
- The feelings your problems generate inside you.
- The behaviour you demonstrate and the actions you subsequently take.

I'll explain more about this in the next few chapters, but what happens when you decide to take control is you release the shackles that have been holding you back. You become receptive to alternative ways of dealing with stress and worry that can bring you great relief. You begin to realise that you really do have a choice about how you're going to respond to the difficulties in your life. And finally, as you start to change the way you respond, your problems transform into something that can be managed and overcome, rather than being show stoppers that undermine your happiness and inner peace.

And if you're thinking it's not possible to change or you're not sure you can do it, please put any doubts on one side for the moment. As a former 5-star worrier, I can vouch for the fact that it really is possible to change the way you think and feel about your problems, and not only find some peace of mind, but also improve the outcomes in your life.

KEY POINTS

1. Worry is very personal. Just because someone else isn't worried about something that's causing you great angst doesn't mean it's not real to you.
2. There are four things that influence the extent to which you worry: your genetic make-up, your upbringing, the experiences you've had in life and your ability to learn new ways of dealing with worrying situations.
3. When you're worried about something, it's because your mind and body have been subjected to something stressful triggered either by the external demands of life or your internal thoughts and feelings. You're concerned whether you can cope with the demands being made on you.
4. The triggers are part of everyday life; you can't avoid them. The key is learning how to manage them.
5. The way forward is to change your response to the difficulties you're facing. This means recognising that you really do have a choice over how you respond. This is done by changing the things over which you have complete control, namely the way you think about your problems, the feelings they generate inside you, the behaviour you then demonstrate and the actions you subsequently take. This has the effect of transforming your problems into something that can be managed and overcome rather than something that drags you down.
6. You really can get relief from your troubles and worries, so for now, please stay open to this possibility, even if you can't imagine how. You can do it; you just need to know what to do and how to do it. And then, it just takes a bit of time and practice.

CHAPTER 2: DISPELLING THE MYTHS ABOUT WORRY

TOO GOOD TO BE TRUE?

You've probably come across people who remain calm and relaxed no matter what's happening in their lives. And I don't just mean those who smile and put a brave face on, but people who really are – deep down – at peace with themselves and what's going on around them.

They're not fazed by the ups and downs of everyday life. They don't let what's happening drag them down or hold them back. They don't bear grudges. They've moved on from any regrets they may have had. And they're not beset with all sorts of doubts and fears. Instead they calmly take everything in their stride, dealing with life's problems in a quietly confident way.

And if you're tempted to think: *it's all right for them, they're not born worriers*, think again. Many of them were born with a tendency to worry and were brought up in a worry focused environment. They too have had their fair share of troubles, and have learnt the hard way.

What's great about the times in which we now live is there's an opportunity to become calm and quietly confident, just like them. Thanks to advances made in the study of the mind, we now know that it really **is** possible to lead a life where you're not dragged down by all sorts of concerns…a life where **you're** in control… where you can rekindle your love of life…where your relationships flourish…where you laugh again…where you experience fulfilment and satisfaction…where you feel calm and peaceful inside…where you restore your well-being…and where you feel genuinely grateful to be alive.

But the question is this: do you believe – really believe – all this is possible?

What I would like to do in this chapter is dispel some of the myths surrounding worry and explain a little bit more about why it's possible to put constant worry behind you once and for all.

MYTH #1: WORRY IS NATURAL

Many people believe that worry is natural, and this is true in the sense that we're hard-wired to respond to the immediate threats in our lives. But this is very different from a tendency to worry about everything and always expect the worst; that is not natural.

When you're exposed to something that's potentially harmful, your body has an in-built mechanism to prepare you for *fight or flight*. This is good news, because it serves you well in an emergency, such as if a bully is threatening to hit you or you need to swerve to avoid another car. But more often than not in your everyday life, the problems you face, together with the heightened state of readiness that goes with them, can't be dissipated by fighting or running away. Consequently, if you're not aware of this, your mind and body tend to remain in a state of continual stress, which can fuel your tendency to worry, as well as having potentially harmful side effects on your physical health.

So, if you have a predisposition to worry about everything and anticipate difficulties at every turn, it's important to curb this inclination, because it actually saps your strength and ability to deal with everyday problems, while at the same time destroying your inner peace.

MYTH #2: WORRY PROTECTS US

Sometimes people think that if you worry about something, you'll be able to cope more easily if or when something bad happens. The logic here is that if you fear the worst, you'll be more prepared to deal with the situation, but in fact the opposite applies. Worry often distracts and immobilises, thereby undermining your ability to cope with what's happening. And it certainly doesn't take away all the emotional pain; it just adds to it.

It's therefore important not to confuse worry with future planning. Fretting about what might happen with fleeting thoughts about what you would do if an unfortunate event were to occur is not the same as thinking through the issues and coming up with a well-thought-out contingency plan.

And another aspect of the belief that worry protects us is the perception that worry somehow prevents something bad from happening. You may have heard people say: *if I stopped worrying, something bad will happen* or *I don't want to tempt fate by not worrying*. But this is simply not true. If you think about it logically, life being what it is, bad things sometimes happen irrespective of whether you worry or not.

So, please don't be tempted to think that worry somehow protects you.

MYTH #3: WORRY HELPS SOLVE OUR PROBLEMS

Occasionally, people think that worry can help solve the problems they're facing, but this is a misunderstanding, because worry and problem solving are two very different things.

Problem solving is a logical process, which involves identifying the key issues, weighing up the pros and cons, brainstorming ideas, reviewing the advantages and disadvantages of possible solutions and then making a considered decision about what to do.

Worry, on the other hand, typically involves going over the problem again and again, often without making much progress. It's frequently accompanied by a sense of feeling overwhelmed or stuck, and if anything, tends to distort your perspective and reduce your ability to really focus on the issues and come up with a real solution.

So, it's important not to confuse worry with problem solving.

MYTH #4: WORRY STOPS US FROM FEELING BAD LATER

Also, there may be a temptation to think that worrying is a bit like making an advance payment, i.e. if you worry about something now, you won't be so upset if a bad thing actually happens in the future. It's as though worrying about a potential problem beforehand minimises, or even stops us from experiencing the upset, disappointment, sadness or hurt later down the line. But it doesn't work like that.

Sadly, experiencing negative emotions is part of life; you simply can't get rid of them by worrying in advance. If something upsetting happens in the future, you're going to be upset, and will need to deal with those emotions at the time, irrespective of whether (or not) you've worried about it beforehand.

MYTH #5: WORRY IS A SIGN OF COMPASSION

Sometimes, there can be a tendency to think that people who worry are more caring and compassionate than those who don't. But is this really true? I don't think it is. There are many people who have a natural concern and care deeply for others without being persistent worriers. If you think about your own loved ones, would they really think you didn't care if you were to stop worrying about them all the time?

There's another aspect to this as well, which is very important. Worry can actually become a burden to the other person, and can even undermine their confidence to deal with life's problems, especially if you're constantly expressing your concerns.

MYTH #6: WORRY IS A GREAT MOTIVATOR

Many people believe that worry helps them accomplish the things they need to get done in their lives. *If I didn't worry about how I look, I'd never exercise regularly. If I didn't worry about my work projects, I'd never get them done on time*. And so on.

But the reality is that worry is actually a demotivator. What happens when you worry is that the pressure starts to build inside and you feel overwhelmed. And when you feel overwhelmed, you can't think so clearly, you're drained of energy, you may be tempted to avoid things and end up getting less (rather than more) things done. So, worry is definitely not a good motivator.

And now we come to the final myth…

MYTH #7: I'VE ALWAYS BEEN A WORRIER AND ALWAYS WILL BE

There are four things that affect the extent to which you worry: your genetic make-up, your upbringing, the experiences you've gone through and, finally, your ability to learn new ways of dealing with life's difficulties, even if you've been a persistent worrier up until now. And it's the last point that's good news for all worriers, because irrespective of what's gone before, it is possible to learn how to deal with stress and worry more effectively.

You don't have to be dragged down by doubts and fears. You really can lead a life where you feel calm, confident and relaxed, knowing that you can deal with whatever comes your way. But, so often the biggest challenge in accomplishing this turnaround is believing – really believing – that you can change and lead a life free from the draining effects of stress and worry.

So, let's talk about that now.

WORRY IS A HABIT

If you're someone who's always been prone to constant worrying – like I used to be – you may be feeling very doubtful about whether you can make the transition from a worrier to a non-worrier. But you can. The reason you may be thinking you can't change is because your predisposition to worry has become a habit that happens so automatically it seems set in stone; one of those things that can't be altered.

Every minute of every day, our minds are active, whether we're preparing a meal, driving, answering emails, talking with our friends or putting our head on the pillow last thing at night. Our mind never stops; it's always processing what's going on around us, what's gone before and what we've got to deal with in the future.

All sorts of deep-seated attitudes and beliefs are stored away in the back of our minds, many of which were developed shortly after we were born and when we were growing up. At that point in our lives, our minds were wide open, and so we absorbed all we were told or what we sensed was going on around us, simply because we were too young to have any way of evaluating things for ourselves.

If we were fortunate enough to have been brought up by people who were positive and confident, the ideas and information they shared with us will have provided a solid grounding for us to step out bravely into the wider world. But if those close to us were fearful and saw the world as a threatening place, their concerns and worries will have become deeply ingrained in us, causing us to be fearful and lacking in confidence.

On top of that, if we then went through challenging experiences as our lives evolved – experiences that we couldn't handle at the time – those events are also likely to have created all sorts of negative attitudes about ourselves and beliefs about what we can and can't accomplish in life.

What this all adds up to is that our attitudes, beliefs and past experiences create a way of looking at the world. They develop into a way of thinking that has become a habit, happening automatically, often without us even realising. As far as we're concerned, the way we think about something is just how it is; it becomes the reality inside our head. And as a result, it **seems** as though we can't change how we think about things, including the extent to which we worry.

But this is an illusion, because we can all change.

YOU HAVE A CHOICE

Worry is like any other habit that's not serving you well; it's possible to break the hold it has on your life, even if you're a constant worrier. You simply need to know what to do and how to do it.

Strange as it may seem, the problem comes not so much from the difficulties you're facing, but from the way **you think and feel about** those difficulties.

When you're consumed with worry, it's very easy to get locked into the idea that you've got no choice and have to accept whatever's happening. It's as though something's being done to you and there's nothing you can do about it. But this is a false impression.

Yes, you might dearly wish that your demanding boss was more reasonable; that your partner hadn't walked out; or that you weren't up to your eyes in debt. Of course, you would prefer these things to be different.

But the truth of the matter is you can't change the way other people behave; only they can do that. And you can't change what's gone before and the situation in which you find yourself. But what you can change is **how you respond right now**. And this is the key to overcoming worry and finding some peace of mind.

So, what does this all mean?

FOCUS ON WHAT YOU CAN CONTROL

When you switch your attention away from the problem to how you can respond, you switch your focus from what you can't control to what you can control, which is empowering. And effectively, there are three things over which you have control; the way you **think** about your problems, the **feelings** they arouse within you and the **actions** you subsequently take.

As mentioned earlier, you can't change what someone else says and does, and you can't change the situation in which you find yourself right now, but you **can** change how you think, feel and behave in response. And this is what makes all the difference when it comes to overcoming worry and its distressing side effects.

So, hopefully, you can now appreciate what needs to be done, but quite rightly, you may well be asking how it can be accomplished. And in order to answer that question, we need to unlock the mystery of the mind, which is covered in the next chapter.

KEY POINTS

1. Constant worry saps your strength and ability to deal with everyday problems, while at the same time destroying your inner peace. It's vital to curb any tendency you may have to worry about everything and anticipate difficulties at every turn.

2. Worry must not be confused with future planning. Agonising about what might happen with fleeting thoughts about what you would do if an unfortunate event were to occur is not the same as thinking through the issues and coming up with a well-thought-out contingency plan.

3. Problem solving is a logical process, which involves weighing up the pros and cons, coming up with possible solutions and then making a considered decision about what to do, whereas worry typically involves churning over the problem again and again, often without making much progress.

4. Worrying about a potential problem in advance does not reduce or stop us from experiencing the upset, disappointment or hurt further down the line.

5. There are many people who care deeply for others without being persistent worriers; just because they don't worry all the time doesn't mean they lack compassion.

6. Worry is a demotivator. If you're constantly turning over your doubts and fears, there is a risk that you'll start to feel overwhelmed. And when you feel overwhelmed, you can't

think so clearly, you're drained of energy, you may be tempted to avoid things and end up getting less done.

7. Everyone has the ability to learn new ways of dealing with life's difficulties, even people who have worried all their lives.

8. Our attitudes, beliefs and past experiences create a way of looking at the world. They develop into a way of thinking that morphs into a habit, happening automatically, often without us even realising. As far as we're concerned, the way we think about something is just how it is, and as a result, it seems as though we can't change the way we think about things, including the extent to which we worry. But this is an illusion.

9. You can't change the way other people behave and you can't change what's gone before, but you can change how you respond. The key is to focus on what you can control, namely the way you think about your problems, the feelings they arouse within you and the actions you subsequently take.

PART 2:
THE KEY TO SUCCESS

CHAPTER 3: UNLOCKING THE MYSTERY OF YOUR MIND

THE KEY TO OVERCOMING WORRY

The challenge for all of us is how to stop our worries from running riot in our minds and undermining all the good things in our lives, especially our happiness, well-being and peace of mind.

When we're angst-ridden and consumed with worry, the problem doesn't come from the stressful situation itself, but from our *response* to the situation. This may be hard to accept, but it explains why, when a group of people is faced with the same difficulty, one of them might be overwhelmed with anxiety, another might be slightly concerned, someone else might see it as a challenge, and yet another couldn't care less.

If we can learn how to change our response to the problems we're facing, we can transform worry into something more manageable… and ease it out of our lives.

But how can we change our response?

Well, the answer to this question lies in doing two things:

- First, by recognising that we really do have a *choice* over how we respond…even if it doesn't always seem like it.
- And secondly, by changing the things we have *control* over, namely our thoughts, feelings and the actions we subsequently take.

This is the key to getting rid of the draining effects of stress and worry, and yet it leads on to another question:

How do we actually change our thoughts, feelings and behaviour?

We might recognise that we have a choice in the matter, we might be willing to make the change, and yet when we do our best not to worry, it seems incredibly difficult to do.

The answer lies in unlocking the mystery of the mind.

What I'd like to do in this chapter and the next is run through some aspects of **how** our mind works and **why** it's important to change the way we think. Then we'll start to explore how you can make the change in your everyday life, so you can smooth away your worries and find some peace of mind.

YOU HAVE A CHOICE...EVEN IF IT DOESN'T FEEL LIKE IT

Even though it may not feel like it right now, you can actually choose the thoughts in your conscious mind, whether they're worry-type thoughts or more upbeat thoughts. The reason it may feel as though you don't have a choice is that the way you think – the way we all think – has become a habit that has built up over a lifetime.

All sorts of deep-seated attitudes and beliefs are stored in our subconscious mind. If these attitudes and beliefs are negative, they can create powerful doubts and worries that affect how we think, feel, the actions we take and ultimately the outcomes we experience. Quite simply, a belief is anything we consider to be true, and includes things like:

- Perceptions we have of ourselves. E.g. what we think we can or can't do, whether we believe we're a worthy person or not.
- Our perceptions of others. E.g. are people generally kind and caring, or are they out to 'get one over on us'?

- How we view life in general and the world around us. E.g. is it a safe or a threatening place? Are there opportunities for everyone or just the 'lucky ones'?
- How we view different aspects of life, such as our family, friends/social skills, romance, work/career, money and health.

What's more, these attitudes and beliefs frequently operate below the radar, so we're often unaware of them and how they're affecting our lives.

HOW NEGATIVE ATTITUDES AND BELIEFS AFFECT OUR LIVES

Because these negative attitudes and beliefs have become deeply ingrained over time, we often don't even notice them, nor do we appreciate the impact they're having. Typically, they influence our lives in three ways.

First, they can lead us to over-generalise and make invalid assumptions. For example, if you're overlooked in the latest round of promotions at work, that doesn't mean you're not good at your job nor worthy of promotion. Many other factors could apply. If you had a bad experience with a romantic partner, it would be very limiting if you then viewed all potential romantic partners in the same way. And if you find yourself shouting at your child at the end of a tiring day, that doesn't automatically make you a bad parent. A good clue as to whether you are over-generalising in an unhelpful way is if you find yourself using words like *everyone, always, no-one* or *never*.

Secondly, negative beliefs can also cause us to misconstrue what's really happening in our lives by unintentionally misinterpreting a situation, or what someone says or does, so that it fits with our perception of other people and the world around us. Have you ever been involved in a heated discussion with several other people only to discover subsequently that everyone has a different perception of what happened and the motivations that were involved? This is because everyone views the situation through a slightly different lens.

Negative beliefs can even cause us to blank out aspects of what's going on around us so that we don't notice certain things, and we don't even realise we're doing it.

This is all very sobering, but the good news is that we can learn to become aware of any negative attitudes and beliefs that may be holding us back, and we can actually change the way we think and feel about things, thus easing doubts and fears. But in order to do this, it's important to understand the link between our conscious and subconscious mind.

THE VITAL LINK BETWEEN OUR CONSCIOUS AND SUB-CONSCIOUS MIND

Our conscious mind is the part of our mind over which we have direct control. It is where our ability to reason and concentrate lives. It can also make choices and has the capacity to **accept or reject** any information that comes our way, although this often takes place so quickly we don't even realise it's happening. The other interesting attribute of our conscious mind is that it's a channel through which we can communicate directly with our subconscious, and the importance of this will soon become apparent.

In contrast, our subconscious is the powerhouse that operates beyond our conscious awareness. It's where the memories of all that's happened in our lives – both good and bad – are stored, along with our attitudes and beliefs that have built up over time. One of its main jobs is to keep a lookout for potential threats so it can keep us safe. This is why, when we're faced with a problem, it may throw up all sorts of doubts and fears through our conscious mind that say: *look out! It's too risky. You can't do that.* And so on.

But what matters, and this is important from the point of view of smoothing away our worries, is that our subconscious simply **accepts** any information it's given by our conscious mind. What this means is that if we can replace the worry-type thoughts in our conscious mind with more upbeat thoughts, we can reprogram our subconscious to adopt constructive attitudes and beliefs that serve us more effectively.

THE POWER OF OUR SUBCONSCIOUS MIND

The subconscious also has an amazing capacity to draw into our lives solutions to the problems we're facing.

When I was growing up, I remember someone saying to me: *be careful what you wish for*. It was the first time I'd heard that old adage and it puzzled me at the time. *Why did I need to be careful*? All my wishes were for things that would bring great happiness.

At that young age, I thought of the word 'wish' in a make-believe way, simply wanting all my dreams to come true. And in one sense, that still applies.

But decades later, after reading hundreds of books and articles about stress management, listening to as many seminars about the topic, and most importantly, experiencing life's ups and downs, I saw that old adage in a different light.

What I hadn't appreciated all those years ago is that anything we constantly focus our minds on – whether it's positive or negative – can be thought of as a wish.

Our subconscious is a truly phenomenal part of our being. It has the ability to **attract** into our lives all sorts of ideas, solutions, people and situations that are in harmony with our dominant thoughts and feelings. Whatever we dwell on in our conscious mind tends to grow. The more we think about something, the more it affects how we feel and behave, and the more likely it will manifest itself in one way or another in our lives. It really is quite extraordinary, and is why we have to be very careful about what we allow into our minds and what we think about.

Have you ever had the experience where you've been faced with a problem and not known what to do, and you asked yourself over and over again: *how can I solve this, how can I solve this*? Then sometime later, apparently out of nowhere…ping…the perfect solution just popped into your head? Well, that's your subconscious at work.

In order to overcome our troubles and worries, we need to switch our conscious thoughts to something more constructive, and as we do this, we begin to get ideas about how we can overcome difficulties we previously thought were impossible.

CAUSE AND EFFECT

The law of cause and effect states that for every outcome, there's a cause, i.e. everything happens for a reason. We are where we are now as a result of things that have happened in the past. But what's not always appreciated is that our thoughts and feelings, as well as our behaviour, upbringing and the experiences we've had, influence the outcomes in our lives. And arguably, our thoughts are the most important influence of all.

What happens is that our thoughts affect both our feelings (i.e. our emotional state) and our behaviour, and ultimately the outcomes in our lives. In fact, our thoughts, feelings and behaviour are all part of a cybernetic loop; that is to say, they are all connected, which means a change in any one of them creates a change in the other two.

Have you ever had the experience where you were so worried about something that it really dragged you down and you were just not able to do anything? You felt totally demoralised and unable to take any action to sort out the problem you were facing. Maybe a friend or close family member then suggested you go out for a few hours for a bit of light relief, and perhaps reluctantly, you agreed to go. Then after a while, you started to feel a bit brighter and things didn't seem quite so bad. Or maybe that friend talked through the problem with you and you suddenly realised there was a way forward you hadn't seen before. You immediately felt much better and were motivated to take action to sort things out.

Prior to the intervention of your friend, your thoughts, feelings and actions (or lack of actions) were just going around and around in a self-perpetuating loop getting nowhere. You were so worried about the problem you were facing, you felt really down. And the more down you felt, the less able you were to take any action to solve the problem. And when you didn't take any action, it caused you to worry even more. And so, it went on. But when you were obliged to do something different, or to start thinking about the problem in a different way, that cycle was broken. When the cycle was broken, you started to see your worries in a different light.

This is just a very simple example of two things:

- First, it demonstrates cause and effect, i.e. how your thoughts affect your feelings, your feelings affect your behaviour, and your behaviour affects the outcomes in your life.
- Secondly, it illustrates how you can break the worry cycle by thinking, feeling or acting differently.

The downside with this particular example, however, is that you can't always rely on the intervention of a friend or family member, and also, the positive effect of this sort of intervention is often short-lived. What's needed is a better understanding of how this cycle works, so you yourself can intervene effortlessly, each and every time, to stop the worrying thoughts, prevent the gloomy feelings and instigate more constructive actions to deal with the problems you're facing...and to do all this so that it has a lasting, uplifting effect.

MIND AND BODY

Recent scientific discoveries have shown that the brain and the body interact very closely with each other via powerful electrochemical signals. If you have worrying or fearful thoughts, your brain triggers the production of chemicals that make you feel worried or fearful. But it doesn't stop there. Your brain continues to monitor how your body is feeling. If it registers via chemical feedback that you are feeling worried, it will generate more worrying thoughts which in turn produce more chemicals that harmonise with your worried physical and emotional state. This results in your mind and body becoming synchronised so that you start to feel the way you think, and think the way you feel in a self-perpetuating loop.

Over time, your mind and body get into the habit of thinking and feeling in the same way. So, if a new worry is triggered, they recognise the signs from before. They immediately tune in and synchronise by repeating and reinforcing the same cycle of worried thoughts and feelings. This, then, has a knock-on effect in terms of the actions you choose to take (or not take) to deal with the problems you're facing, and as a result, the outcomes you experience.

There is, however, light at the end of the tunnel. In the same way that your brain triggers the production of chemicals that make you feel worried when you have worrying thoughts, it can also trigger chemicals that make you feel happy or peaceful if you have happy or relaxing thoughts. What this means is that you can break the worry habit by changing the content of your thoughts and feelings.

CHANGE IN FOCUS

The key is to switch your thoughts from what you don't want (the worry) to what you do want (the ideal outcome). We will cover exactly how to do this in the next two chapters.

As you start to focus your thoughts on the ideal outcome, your brain triggers the production of chemicals that make you feel more hopeful and upbeat. This in turn encourages more upbeat thoughts, which reinforce the upbeat feelings, and so the cycle continues.

At the same time, your subconscious recognises that you're now focusing on something different, and so gets to work finding a solution to the problem you're facing. New ideas pop into your conscious mind that would previously have been filtered out by your deep-seated attitudes and beliefs. You become aware of all sorts of opportunities and choices you didn't notice before. And most importantly, you start to realise you have skills and qualities you thought you didn't have. Together, these things create a new understanding of yourself and the world around you, enabling you to overcome the difficulties in your life rather than being overwhelmed by your doubts and fears.

These things also affect your behaviour, because you're then motivated to take different sorts of action to resolve the problems you're facing. And when this happens, you start to see real, positive change manifest itself in your external life, leading to more favourable outcomes.

This isn't make-believe; it's a manifestation of how the mind and body work together. What is in fact happening is that when you change your thoughts and feelings, and synchronise the two, you are 'vibrating' at a different level and so are open to new possibilities in your life.

The more you focus on **what you want** rather than on your worries, and the more you start thinking and feeling in terms of what you **can do** rather than what you can't do, you set up a force field of energy that draws new ideas and solutions into your conscious mind. This motivates you to **take action** to resolve the problems you're facing, which in turn moves you in the direction you want to go.

There are some wonderful benefits to taking this approach. First, you discover that your worst fears seldom materialise; as they say, the anticipation is often worse than the event itself. Second, if something awful does happen, more often than not, you find you can deal with it. Third, your self-confidence starts to grow as you realise you can handle difficulties that would previously have immobilised you. Fourth, your creativity, problem-solving abilities and decision-making skills all improve.

And finally, you become calm and more relaxed because you know, deep down inside, you can deal effectively with whatever problems come your way.

By thinking, feeling and behaving differently, your troubles and worries no longer weigh you down or hold you back.

BUT I'VE TRIED TO STOP WORRYING BEFORE AND IT DIDN'T WORK

Now you may be thinking: *that's all very well, but I've tried to stop worrying in the past, and it just doesn't work.* Well, it likely didn't work for one of two reasons.

If you've always worried, your mind and body will have got into a certain way of thinking and feeling that kicks in automatically when you're concerned about something. Because this happens on a subconscious level, you don't even realise what's going on; it's seems as though it's just the way it is. So, when you try 'not to worry' without fully appreciating what's happening under the surface, it feels like it's impossible to change.

Added to this is the fact that you – like all of us – have deep-seated attitudes and beliefs about yourself and the world around you that influence the way you think and feel about things. If many of these beliefs are negative, they reinforce the tendency to worry. Because they're operating on a subconscious level, you don't realise the powerful, adverse effect they're having.

But when you start to understand how the mind and body work together, as well as recognising any deep-seated beliefs you have that may be holding you back, you can start to change the way you deal with the problems in your life and get some relief from your troubles and worries.

I'm mindful that we've covered a lot of new ground in this chapter, so if it doesn't make perfect sense, just accept that for now. It will become clearer as time goes on.

KEY POINTS

1. Even though it may not feel like it right now, you can choose the thoughts in your conscious mind, whether they're worry-type thoughts or more upbeat thoughts.
2. All sorts of deep-seated attitudes and beliefs are stored in your subconscious mind. If they're negative, they can create powerful doubts and worries that affect how you think, feel and behave, and ultimately, the outcomes you experience in your life.

3. Because any negative attitudes and beliefs have become deeply ingrained over time, you often don't even notice them, nor appreciate the impact they are having. The good news is you can learn to become aware of them and how they may be holding you back.
4. The conscious mind is the part of your mind over which you have direct control. It can reason, make choices, accept or reject any information that comes your way, and is also the channel through which you can communicate directly with your subconscious.
5. In contrast, the subconscious is the powerhouse that operates beyond your conscious awareness. It's where the memories of all that's happened in your life are stored, along with attitudes and beliefs that have built up over time. One of its main jobs is to keep a lookout for potential threats so it can keep you safe, which is why, when you're faced with a problem, it may throw up all sorts of doubts and fears through your conscious mind that say: *look out! It's too risky. You can't do that.* However, it also has an amazing capacity to draw into your life solutions to the problems you're facing.
6. The subconscious simply accepts any information it's given by the conscious mind, which means if you can replace the worry-type thoughts in your conscious mind with more constructive thoughts, you can reprogram the subconscious to adopt constructive attitudes and beliefs that serve you more effectively.
7. Recent scientific discoveries have shown that the brain and the body interact very closely with each other via powerful electrochemical signals. If you have worrying or fearful thoughts, your brain triggers the production of chemicals that make you feel worried or fearful. Conversely, it can also trigger chemicals that make you feel happy or peaceful if you have happy or relaxing

thoughts. What this means is that you can break the worry habit by changing your thoughts and feelings.

8. Your thoughts, feelings and behaviour are all part of a cybernetic loop, which means they are all connected. A change in any one of them creates a change in the other two. As you start to adopt more constructive thoughts in your conscious mind, this has a positive knock-on effect emotionally, physically and behaviourally, leading to more satisfactory outcomes.
9. The key is to switch your thoughts from what you don't want (the worry) to what you do want (the ideal outcome). This has the effect of causing you to feel more upbeat, and new ideas about how to solve your problems (that would previously have been filtered out by your deep-seated attitudes and beliefs) pop into your head. You're then motivated to take action to resolve these difficulties, leading to more favourable outcomes.

QUESTIONS

In order to help you become more aware of any deep-seated attitudes and beliefs that may be generating doubts and worries in your mind, and holding you back, I recommend answering the questions below. They are designed to help bring any underlying negative beliefs out into the open, so you become more aware of them, how they trigger doubt and worry, and how they're affecting your life.

A belief is simply something you consider to be true, and includes things like the perceptions you have of yourself and other people, how you view the world around you, and how you view different aspects of life such as family, friends/social skills, romance, work/career, money and health.

If you're like the rest of us, you will probably have a blend of both positive and negative beliefs about these things, so don't be tempted to write down just the good points! And please don't record attitudes or beliefs that you feel you ought to have. Be honest with yourself, because that's the only way you will become consciously aware of what you really believe in important areas of your life.

I suggest spending 20-30 minutes jotting down the answers that come into your mind, then leave it for a few days before coming back to add any further thoughts. Often different ideas come into your mind if you give your subconscious time to think things over. It's important to write (or type) out your answers as fully as you can rather than just mulling them over in your head, because writing helps clarify your thoughts and gives you greater insight.

Keep in mind, there are no right or wrong answers. The key is just to get a better understanding of any negative beliefs that may be causing you to doubt or worry. Your answers will then provide a benchmark you can use to monitor your progress going forward.

1a What do you believe about yourself? (E.g. What are your qualities and perceived shortcomings? What do you believe you can and can't do? Do you believe you are a worthy person? If not, why not?)

1b Have any of your beliefs about yourself caused you to worry or have doubts about what you can do? If so, in what way?

2a What do you believe about other people? (E.g. What are the qualities and shortcomings of other people? Do your beliefs vary if you're thinking about total strangers, authority figures, work colleagues, family members, romantic partners or friends? If so, how?)

2b Have any of your beliefs about other people caused you to worry or have doubts about yourself? If so, in what way? (E.g. Do you believe that someone who has spent longer in full-time education than you is more capable? Do you consider that people who have a higher salary are more successful?)

3a How do you view the world around you and life in general? (E.g. Do you see the world as a safe or a dangerous place? Why do you say that? Is life filled with opportunities or problems? Is it a challenge or a breeze? In what way?)

3b Have any of your beliefs about the world and life in general caused you to worry? If so, in what way?

4a Are there any areas of your life that you are worried about? If so, which ones? (E.g. Family, friends/social skills, romance, work/career, money and health.)
For each area of your life that you are worried about, ask yourself the following questions:

4b What do you believe about <area of life>?

4c How have your beliefs about <area of life> caused you to worry?

CHAPTER 4: POWER OF INTERNAL DIALOGUE AND PICTURES

RUNNING ON AUTOPILOT

Much of the time in our daily lives, our minds run on autopilot. We go from one thought to the next, often at great speed and there can be a tendency to assume there's nothing that can be done to stop this free-flow of thoughts, particularly if they're worrying ones. But this is an illusion.

Right now, you may still be wondering whether it really is possible to change the way you think, and get some relief from all your worries – that's certainly how I felt at one time – but the fact is, you can; it just takes a bit of time and practice to replace old worry habits with something more effective.

When we're in a state of constant worry, we become very apprehensive and often feel down and demoralised. And when we're in this emotional state, it's very difficult to get motivated to take action to solve the problems we're facing. Then, when we don't take any action, nothing changes, which causes us to worry even more, and so it goes on in a negative, self-perpetuating cycle.

But the good news is that we can break this worry cycle by doing two things. First of all, by switching our thoughts and feelings to something more upbeat, and secondly, by reprogramming our subconscious to adopt more constructive attitudes and beliefs, as well as come up with possible solutions to the difficulties we're facing. And the way to do this is by changing the worry thoughts in our conscious mind to something more constructive; what I think of as focusing our conscious mind on the ideal outcome, i.e. what we would like to happen if everything were to work out perfectly. As we do that, we start to feel more upbeat and get ideas about how we can overcome difficulties we previously thought were impossible. Then, when we see a way forward, we feel more energised and take action to resolve those difficulties. This, in turn, leads to more positive outcomes, and we start to think and behave in a more calm and confident manner. And then the cycle continues, but in a more constructive way.

BECOMING MORE AWARE

Literally thousands of thoughts cross our mind every day, but many of them flash by so quickly, we don't even register them. Therefore, the first task is to become more aware of what you spend your time thinking about.

And in order to do this, you need to have a clear understanding of exactly what a thought is, because thinking takes several different forms. The first one – the one we're most familiar with – is our self-talk, which is the dialogue that goes on inside our head, as we consider everything that's happening in our lives. You know the sort of thing I mean. *What if I'm late? Will Mary still be there? How will I find her?* And so on. But we also think in pictures that we see on the screen in our mind, and in sounds (or tone of voice) we hear inside our head. So, in the example I've just given, my tone of voice might be slightly anxious, as I'm saying these worrying things to myself, accompanied by a picture in my mind's eye in which Mary is nowhere to be seen. At the same time, I might also be feeling tension in some part of my body.

Thoughts are actually a combination of internal dialogue, pictures and tone of voice, which together form a very powerful means of communicating messages to our subconscious.

Noticing what goes on inside your head takes a bit of practice at first, because much of what happens, happens automatically, in fact, almost unconsciously. Thoughts flash across your internal radar, and are gone before you even have a chance to register them. You're just left with the residual concern or worry.

So, let's take a closer look at exactly what's happening.

INTERNAL DIALOGUE

When people talk about 'thinking', they're often referring to the internal dialogue that goes on inside. I don't know whether you've ever noticed that there's an almost constant stream of self-talk going on all the time. If you've ever tried to make your mind go blank and not to think about anything, you may have noticed that it's virtually impossible, because within seconds, something flashes into your mind. This is really important, because the words you say to yourself can lift you up or put you down, they can make you happy or sad, they can shroud you in worry or help free you from your concerns, but in order for this to happen, you need to become aware of the content of this internal dialogue.

What tends to happen when you're worried about something is that you have a constant stream of negative thoughts that help create and reinforce a state of worry. These thoughts may be related to something that happened in the past, or to something that might happen in the future.

- Reliving the past via your conscious mind may include thoughts like: *why did I have to make a mistake? If only he hadn't walked out. It's not fair that I lost my job. What's the point, it won't work out like before?* And other such thoughts.

- Pre-living the future may involve thoughts such as: *I can't do it. What if I can't pay the bills? I always make a fool of myself. There's too much to do, I can't cope.* And so on.

Because these thoughts run on autopilot, you're often unaware of just how much you focus on them. And the more you focus on them, the more worried you become. One of the aims of this book is to help bring these negative thoughts and associated feelings to the front of your mind, so you become more conscious of – and therefore can change – what you're actually saying to yourself. This is a key element of dealing with your worries. But before we discuss how to do this in Chapter 5, I want to talk a bit more about what is meant by 'thinking'.

Our internal dialogue (or self-talk) is indeed one mode of thinking that affects the extent to which we worry, but there are others, which are linked to our senses and which we also need to take into account.

THE PICTURES ON THE SCREEN IN OUR MIND

One of the most important modes of thinking relates to our visual capacity, which plays a key role in the context of worry, as we have an extraordinary ability to create pictures or movies inside our head. Often our internal dialogue is accompanied by very vivid pictures of what we're worried about or what might go wrong, which reinforces the worry we're experiencing. What's interesting though is that these internal pictures can flash by very quickly, so we may be totally unaware of them. But even if we're unaware of them, that doesn't mean they're not having an impact. And in the case of pictures that are reinforcing worry, they can have a very negative effect.

It took me a long time to realise that the pictures on the internal screen in my mind were even there, and having a huge impact on the way I thought and felt. To begin with, I was so focused on the conversation going on inside my head, I didn't even notice the pictures that accompanied the words. Then I gradually started to become aware of them and realised the profound effect they were having on how I felt.

You may have heard the expression *a picture paints a thousand words.* It's so true. Literally, in the blink of an eye, your mind can generate a picture that conjures up and reinforces happy feelings, sad feelings, worry, and any other number of different feelings.

If I say to you, 'picture your home', a picture of your home immediately comes into your mind. If I then say, 'picture a close friend', again a picture of that person comes into your mind. Equally, if I say, 'picture something you're worried about, like being unwell, not having enough money or having a difficult conversation with your boss', I bet a picture of that flashes into your mind as well. Much of the time, you're just not consciously aware of these internal pictures, let alone the impact they're having, whether good or bad.

You need, however, to keep in mind that the pictures you see inside your head may not be quite the same as when you look at something outside yourself. They can have all sorts of different characteristics. By this, I mean they may be still or moving, if they're moving, they can be fast or slow, they may be large or small, framed or taking up your whole internal field of vision. They may be in front of you or to one side, they may be focused or unfocused, bright or dim, in colour or black and white, and finally, they may be associated or dissociated, where associated means you're looking through your own eyes, while dissociated means you're looking at yourself in the picture.

To begin with, you probably won't notice all these details, and that's fine, because it takes a bit of practice to become aware of all the nuances. Just do your best to notice the content of the pictures on the screen in your mind when you are worried about something, and as time goes on, you'll start to notice these other characteristics as well. With a bit more practice, you may find that the nuances vary depending on whether you're feeling upbeat or down, happy or sad, fired up or weary, and so on.

THE SOUNDS INSIDE OUR HEAD

The next thinking mode I'd like to explore relates to our auditory capacity. Sounds inside our head can take many different forms, both positive and negative. They may be very distinctive like a shout, a scream or a cry for help, but they can also be much more subtle, like an anxious, helpless, desperate, critical, impatient or demanding tone of voice that we use when talking to ourselves, or when recalling or imagining a conversation with someone else. We may also be speaking with a slow, weary voice or using a loud, rapid-fire style. And just as we discussed in the context of the pictures that flash across our mind, these distinctive sounds or tones can have a huge impact in terms of initiating or reinforcing a worried state of mind if they are negative sounds. The problem, however, is that we're not always aware of them. They just 'happen' and, if they're negative, can trigger or accentuate our predisposition to worry.

What's more, these sounds or tones of voice also have different characteristics. They may be loud or soft, clear or distorted, fast or slow, high or low in pitch, continuous or with pauses, coming from a particular direction, close by or far away. And as with the pictures inside our head, it can take time to become more aware of these different characteristics, so just start to notice what you can about the sounds or tones of voice you use when you're worried, and how they may differ to when you're feeling calm and relaxed. The more you practice, the more aware you will become of these different nuances.

OUR ABILITY TO SENSE TENSION (OR OTHER FEELINGS) INSIDE OUR BODY

Next, I want to mention our ability to sense what's happening in various parts of our body, sometimes referred to as our kinaesthetic intelligence or physical reaction. Often worry is accompanied and aggravated by tension in the neck and shoulders or tightness across the chest, but there can be any number of physical reactions that affect your body when you're worried. It's different for different people. A feeling may have a particular location in your body, it may have a particular shape and size, may stay in one place or move around, be hot or cold, steady or pulsating, and be light or heavy. Worry can also manifest itself in a variety of other signs such as a dry mouth or a lump in your throat, rapid heartbeat or breathlessness, headaches, a pain in your neck, shoulders or back, shaking hands, a churning stomach or tiredness. Alternatively, you might feel hot and flushed, or sick or dizzy.

Increased awareness includes noticing what is happening to you physically, as well as becoming more aware of the dialogue, pictures and sounds going on inside your head. I came to realise that whenever I was anxious about something, I would tense my body, particularly my neck and shoulders. Even now, I can catch myself doing it unawares. So, a worried state of mind can also be accompanied by a changed physical state.

As an aside, I need to highlight that some of these signs can be indicative of an underlying illness rather than worry, so if you are experiencing some of these symptoms and are in any doubt about the cause, you must consult a qualified medical professional.

IMPACT ON OUR EMOTIONAL STATE AND BEHAVIOUR

You may remember from the previous chapter that our mind and body interact with each other using electrochemical signals. When you have worry-type thoughts, your brain triggers the production of chemicals that affect your body with the result that you start to feel worried. If you continue to feel worried, your brain then generates more worry-type thoughts, and so it carries on with the result that your mind, body and the associated emotions become synchronised in a worry loop.

Keep in mind that worry-type thoughts and feelings are many and varied. We've already spoken about a sense of not being in control or having no choice, but worry can also manifest itself as feelings of isolation or inadequacy, lack of confidence, guilt, rejection, suspicion, and feelings of being under attack or tearful. It can encompass not knowing how to deal with a situation, being afraid of making a mistake or taking a risk and anticipating the worst. There may also be a tendency to become impatient, irritable, short-tempered, aggressive or resentful. None of these manifestations are good for your mental, physical and emotional well-being.

However, not only do our thoughts affect our feelings, and our feelings affect our thoughts, but these two together also affect our behaviour, and ultimately the outcomes in our lives.

When we're locked into a state of worry, our thoughts and feelings can lead to all sorts of unhelpful behaviours such as procrastination, a tendency to avoid difficult situations and social contact or not taking the necessary action to resolve problems. It may also encompass not getting through as many tasks as usual, poor time keeping, making mistakes and being defensive, as well as eating and drinking more than usual.

The knock-on effects of worry are therefore considerable.

THE IMPORTANCE OF DIFFERENT THINKING MODES

Our different thinking modes, as well as the physical reaction in our bodies, all complement and reinforce one another. Together, they influence our emotional state and behaviour, which in turn affect what happens in our external world. This is why, when trying to get rid of the worry in our lives, it's essential to become aware of – and then change – not only our internal dialogue, but also the tone of voice we use and the internal pictures that flash across the screen in our mind.

SWITCHING FROM UNCONSCIOUS TO CONSCIOUS THINKING

The first step in smoothing away your worries and finding some peace of mind is therefore to become consciously aware of how worry manifests itself in your life, which means becoming aware of your thoughts, feelings and behaviour when you're faced with a problem and concerned about the possible outcome.

The process for becoming more aware of what's going on in your conscious mind is simply to **start noticing what you say to yourself, the tone of voice you use and any pictures you create in your mind's eye, as well as any physical reactions you may experience in your body and the effect this all has on your emotional state and behaviour**. The chances are, like most people, your thoughts have probably been running on autopilot for most of your life, so it can take a bit of practice to become fully aware of these different things, as it all flashes by so quickly. Be patient with yourself; don't get annoyed or upset, or start to think you can't do it if you don't master it right away. Just stay with it, and as you do, you'll gradually notice more and more of what's going on inside.

Then with a bit more practice, you'll start to appreciate how not only the content of your thoughts, but also their **typical characteristics vary** depending on whether you're worried or calm and relaxed. And by this, I mean whether your internal pictures are still or moving, bright or dull, in colour or black and white, and so on. Also, whether your tone of voice is anxious or demanding, helpless or impatient, loud or soft, fast or slow, etc.

Ultimately, you'll start to notice the **sequence in which your thoughts appear.** For instance, whether the self-talk comes before the internal picture and physical reactions, or whether the picture comes first. The sequence may also vary depending on what you are thinking about.

Please note, I'm simply asking you to notice what's going on inside; I'm not asking you to analyse it or to try and attach any meaning to it. Just go inside and notice what's happening.

Once you become more aware of how you 'do' worry, (i.e. what you say to yourself, the tone of voice you use and the pictures that flash across your mind, as well as how this affects your emotional state and behaviour), you can then start to change what you do inside.

Three important things occur when you change the content of your worry-type thoughts to something more constructive. First, the chemical signals between your brain and body change, so that as you start to have happy, upbeat thoughts, you begin to feel happy and upbeat, with the result that your mind and body become synchronised in a more constructive way. Secondly, you start to develop a new understanding of yourself and the world around you. You often discover you have skills and qualities you didn't know you had, and you become more confident about dealing with life's problems. And thirdly, you fire up your subconscious to go off and find solutions to the difficulties you're facing.

It took me a long while to get my head around how this all works, so if you're finding that it doesn't make complete sense right now, just accept that for the time being. It will come together as you start to put these concepts into practice.

KEY POINTS

1. Much of the time our minds run on autopilot. Literally thousands of thoughts cross our mind every day, but many of them flash by so quickly, we don't even register them.
2. There are several different modes of thinking: our internal dialogue (or self-talk), the pictures on the screen in our mind, and the tone of voice we use or sounds we hear inside our head. Our thoughts are also accompanied by different physical reactions in our body.
3. The words we say to ourselves can lift us up or put us down, they can make us happy or sad, they can shroud us in worry or help free us from concern.
4. Often our internal dialogue is accompanied by vivid pictures of what we're worried about, which reinforces the worry we're experiencing. Frequently, these internal pictures flash by so quickly, we may not even be aware of them.
5. The tone of voice we use when talking to ourselves reinforces the words we use and the pictures we create inside our mind.
6. The physical reactions associated with worry are many and varied, and differ from person to person. It is important not to confuse these signs with the symptoms of an underlying illness.

7. The first step in overcoming worry is to become consciously aware of how it manifests itself in your life, which means becoming aware of your thoughts, feelings and behaviour when faced with a problem and concerned about the possible outcome.

8. The process for becoming more aware of what's going on in your conscious mind is simply to start noticing what's going on inside. This means becoming fully cognisant with what you say to yourself when you're worried, the tone of voice you use and any pictures that flash across the screen in your mind, as well as recognising how worry affects you physically, emotionally and in terms of the actions you decide to take (or not take).

9. Three important things occur when you change the content of your worry-type thoughts to something more constructive.
   (a) The chemical signals between your brain and body change, so that as you start to have happy, upbeat thoughts, you begin to feel happy and upbeat, causing your mind and body to become synchronised in a more constructive way.
   (b) You start to develop a new understanding of yourself, and often discover you have skills and qualities you didn't know you had, and you become more confident about dealing with life's problems.
   (c) You fire up your subconscious to go off and find solutions to the difficulties you're facing.

QUESTIONS

To help identify how worry manifests itself in your life, I suggest taking some time over the next few days to answer the questions below.

Start by making a note of the two or three things you're most worried about. There may be more things on your mind, but just focus on what's taking up most of your worry time right now. Then, for each one, answer the following questions. It may help to refer back to the answers you gave to the questions at the end of Chapter 3, particularly when considering why you are worried.

Think about each question and write (or type) out whatever comes into your mind. Trust those thoughts. There are no right or wrong answers, and if you don't know how to respond to one of the questions, that's fine.

Don't expect to notice everything that's going on inside from the word go, it takes time to recognise what's actually happening, but with a little bit of time and practice, you'll master it.

1. What are you worried about?
2. Why are you worried about it?
3. How does your worry affect your thoughts?
    a. Your internal dialogue.
    b. The pictures on the screen in your mind.
    c. The tone of voice you use, or other sounds you hear.
4. What sort of physical reactions do you experience in your body when you are worried?
5. How does worry affect your emotional state?
6. How does it affect your behaviour?
7. What is your level of worry? (Use a 1-5 scale, where 1 = not very worried and 5 = very worried)

Once you've answered the questions for each of your main worries, you'll have a much better understanding of how problems and difficulties manifest themselves in your life.

Then take some time to review what you've written and identify any patterns, in terms of the thoughts, feelings and behaviours you tend to adopt when faced with worrying situations. You may discover that there is a pattern in the way you respond to demanding situations, or you may find you respond to different problems in different ways. The important thing in learning how to manage your troubles and worries more effectively is to become aware of how worry affects you.

CHAPTER 5: THE 5-STEP PROCESS

THE 5-STEP PROCESS: FOCUS ON WHAT YOU WANT

When you find yourself absorbed in your troubles and worries, you need to switch your thoughts to the polar opposite, i.e. what you want rather than what you don't want. For example, if you're feeling lonely, you need to think about having a good circle of caring friends or a romantic partner. If you're worried that you can't do something, you need to think about successfully carrying out the very thing you fear. Or if you're worried about being in debt, you need to think about having enough money to meet your needs.

As you start to focus your thoughts on what you want (i.e. your ideal outcome), your brain triggers the production of chemicals that make you feel more hopeful, upbeat and able to deal with the problems you're facing. It also fires up your subconscious to go off and find a way of resolving your concerns and creating what you want.

It's therefore important to keep your conscious mind focused on your ideal outcome, and the 5-step process outlined in this chapter is designed to help you do that.

1. Recognise the signs of worry
2. Take control of your internal dialogue and the tone of voice you use
3. Create upbeat pictures in your mind
4. Feel the feeling
5. Take action!

The great thing about this approach is that it empowers you and you're no longer held back by old worry habits. You don't have to put up with mind-numbing worries anymore, because you can take positive steps to deal with your concerns, and then reap a happier, more peaceful life.

I hope you had an opportunity to answer the questions at the end of Chapter 4, because when you have a clear understanding of how worry affects you, it's easier to put into practice the steps we'll be covering in this chapter. So, if you haven't had a chance to answer those questions, I suggest doing that before continuing.

STEP 1: RECOGNISE THE SIGNS OF WORRY

The first step in managing your worries more effectively is simply to become more aware of when you're dwelling on your worries, i.e. what you *don't* want.

If you're someone who tends to worry a lot or you've experienced a gradual build-up of stress over a long period of time, the chances are you won't always notice when you're preoccupied with life's problems. This is because worrying has become the norm, and it's only when something is *extremely* worrying do you actually notice that you're spending huge amounts of time dwelling on the problems in your life.

There are six tell-tale signs to help you recognise when you're preoccupied with your troubles and worries:

1. The first clue is that you find yourself using a lot of negative words in your internal dialogue; words like *can't, don't, won't, ought to, shouldn't, never, always, no-one, hopeless, impossible, awful, terrible* or *what if <something> goes wrong?*

2. Secondly, the tone of voice you use when talking to yourself may be anxious, helpless or desperate, or possibly critical, impatient or angry. And you may be speaking to yourself using a slow, weary tone or a loud, rapid-fire style.
3. Next, 'bad news' pictures may be flashing across the screen in your mind, reinforcing your negative self-talk.
4. Your worries may also manifest themselves as a physical reaction in your body, such as tightness or tension.
5. As you tune in to your emotions, you may become aware that you're feeling down, isolated, self-absorbed, guilty, rejected, inadequate or lacking in confidence.
6. And finally, worry may cause you to delay or avoid taking action that might be helpful.

You won't necessarily experience all of these signs, although keep in mind that, to begin with, some may flash by without you even registering them. If this happens, so be it. Just do your best to notice what's going on inside; the more you do this, the more you'll start to recognise the signs of worry.

And if it takes you a bit of time to register that you're even preoccupied with your troubles and worries, be okay with that. What you're trying to do here is change a habit that has built up over the years, so it will take a bit of practice to notice when you're dwelling on your worries. To begin with, what's likely to happen is that you'll be so preoccupied with your doubts and concerns, it will take some time before you even realise you're dwelling on them. After a while, you'll become aware a bit more quickly. And finally, you'll be able to notice worry-type thoughts as soon as they enter your conscious mind, so you can nip them in the bud and stop them from taking root.

STEP 2: TAKE CONTROL OF YOUR INTERNAL DIALOGUE AND THE TONE OF VOICE YOU USE

The second step in getting your worries under control is to stop your mind from continually dwelling on all the problems in your life. Whenever you notice you're preoccupied with your worries, (i.e. what you **don't** want), you need to switch your internal dialogue to the polar opposite, (i.e. what you **do** want). It can be quite difficult to 'hold' what you want in your mind, so to help with this, there are three techniques you can use.

Ask a Question

If you have no idea how to solve the difficulties you're facing, perhaps because you've not come across them before, or because there are so many complexities, ask yourself the *how can I...?* question. *How can I find more friends? How can I find the love of my life? How can I get a promotion? How can I earn more money? How can I improve my health and well-being?*

What happens when you ask the question is that you're giving your subconscious a specific instruction to go off and find the answer. Your subconscious has an amazing capacity to come up with solutions to the problems you're facing, and not just any old solution, but often the perfect solution. So, ask the question and trust that a way forward will be provided. The answer will most likely pop into your head when you're least expecting it. Please don't get angry or upset though, if the answer doesn't come right away; sometimes it will appear the following morning, or it might be a week or a month later. If there's a delay, just repeat the question, trust that a solution will be provided, and then go about your daily life.

This isn't just some flaky idea. Your subconscious is linked to (or is part of) what's often called Infinite Intelligence or the Super-Conscious Mind. And Infinite Intelligence can be thought of as the knowledge of the entire universe; it's the source of all hunches, intuition, inspiration and creativity, and as such, can compute the ideal solution to the problems you're facing. I've lost track of the number of times over the years I've gone to bed wondering how I was going to solve a particular problem and then sometime later… ping…the answer just popped into my head.

It is also important that you trust – really trust – that in asking a question, Infinite Intelligence will provide an answer, and draw a solution into your life.

Use the 'right' vocabulary

When you switch your thoughts to your ideal outcome, you need to choose your words carefully. For example, if you're feeling lonely, it's no good saying to yourself: *I don't want to be lonely anymore,* instead you need to say: *I want a good circle of friends.* This may sound like I'm splitting hairs, but the distinction is crucial, because of the way the subconscious works.

The subconscious mind is more than able to come up with solutions to the problems you're facing, but it needs to be given a very clear message via your conscious mind. If you say: *I don't want to be lonely*, in order to think about '**not** being lonely', your subconscious has first to focus on '**being lonely**'. Think of it like this: it doesn't get the **'not'** part of the request. Instead, it just homes in on **'lonely'**, and there's a real risk you will continue to get 'being lonely'. So, in this example, you need to think about having a good circle of friends.

Create an appropriate affirmation

Affirmations are an extension of using the 'right' vocabulary, and are a way of switching your thoughts to what you want, and keeping them off what you don't want. As you may know, affirmations are short, upbeat messages that you send to your subconscious mind (in this case) to help reduce stress and worry, and bring about positive change in your life. This is done is by saying these phrases to yourself, as you become aware of your mind dwelling on your worries. Think of it as inoculating your doubts and concerns.

What affirmations do is gradually change the way you think and feel about things. Troubles and worries that were previously causing you stress and holding you back are replaced with a new outlook that helps facilitate positive change in your life; change you not only feel 'on the inside', but change that starts to manifest itself 'on the outside' in your external life.

The starting point is to identify the main worries you want to change in your life, and then create a short, upbeat affirmation to inoculate each one, using three basic guidelines.

Each affirmation must:

a. Be personal (i.e. it includes the words 'I' or 'my')

b. Focus on your ideal outcome

c. Be in the present tense

The reason for including the words 'I' or 'my' is that they are deeply personal and empowering.

Creating an affirmation that focuses on your ideal outcome means using words that encapsulate what you *want* rather than what you *don't want.* For example, *I have* ***enough money*** *to meet all my needs* rather than *I'm no longer in* ***debt***. On the face of it, these two statements mean much the same thing, but as far as your subconscious mind is concerned, there's a huge difference between the two. I hope this distinction is clear, but if not, I suggest referring to the list of typical affirmations in the Appendix, because they help emphasise the distinction.

Your chosen affirmation needs to be in the present tense rather than the future tense, because your subconscious doesn't distinguish between the world of the mind and the physical world in which we live. For example, say: *I **have** enough money to meet all my needs,* rather than *I **will have** enough money to meet all my needs.* When you say: *I **have** enough money to meet all my needs*, your subconscious treats this as the truth and sets about helping to make it a reality. In fact, one of the aims of your subconscious is to synchronise your inner and outer worlds.

Only you can choose affirmations – and their exact wording – that are right for you. You may find the perfect one for you in the Appendix, or more likely, you'll want to tailor a few of them or even create something totally different. The key is to choose words that really resonate with you. Don't opt for over-the-top phrases or flowery language that you think you ought to use. Find a way of expressing what you want using the sort of vocabulary you would normally use. The wording has got to feel 'right' for you.

Use a complementary tone of voice

You need to use a tone of voice that 'fits' the affirmation you're working on. It may be an excited tone, a confident tone, or a calm and relaxed tone; whatever is appropriate for each of your affirmations. Try to resist any tendency to say your affirmations like an automaton. Instead, say them with conviction, as though you truly believe what you're saying. This is important because your subconscious picks up on the sentiment behind the words you're saying. If you speak hesitantly, or in a dull and boring voice, your subconscious is going to doubt whether you're really serious about your affirmations and accomplishing what they represent.

Step on your mental accelerator

There's far more to using affirmations than just thinking up what you want to say.

First of all, I encourage you to write your affirmations down and then re-read them at the start and end of the day, as well as focusing your mind on them as often as you can during the course of the day, such as when you're preparing a meal, taking a shower, driving, waiting for an appointment and especially when you find yourself thinking about your worries. It also helps if you say them out loud, whenever possible.

As you start to read or say your new affirmations, it may feel a bit uncomfortable at first, and you might find yourself thinking: *this isn't true*. This is because your deep-seated beliefs about yourself, other people and the world around you that evolved when you were growing up are trying to stop you from changing and developing a more resourceful way of leading your life. This may sound crazy, but it's because your old beliefs and your old way of thinking and feeling have got you safely to this point in your life, so there is going to be some resistance when you try to change your thoughts. But if you persist with your new affirmations, you'll start to impress them on your subconscious and will soon begin to believe they really are true and can become a reality in your life.

The key point about all of this is that when you think fervently about something, you give enormous power to the thought, which in turn affects your feelings and the actions you subsequently take. So, for instance, if you worry about *not* being able to do something, not only does it make you feel rather fearful and discourage you from even trying, the worry also increases your chances of *not* being able to do it, because you think you can't. Conversely, if you focus your thoughts on the polar opposite (i.e. how you *can* do something), it causes you to notice possibilities you didn't think were there before, you realise you have skills you didn't think you had, you feel more upbeat and so step out bravely to accomplish what you want.

Sometimes, it can be difficult to 'hold' a positive affirmation in your conscious mind for any length of time. This is partly because your mind is being continually stimulated – and distracted – by what's going on around you, but also because your mind has got into the habit of always dwelling on your worries. Don't be surprised if this happens, and don't let it discourage you. It doesn't mean you can't break the worry habit. Just bring your thoughts gently back to the new affirmation you want to instil in your mind. It may take a little bit of effort to begin with, but it's worth it, because taking control of your internal dialogue is a key step in freeing you from mind-numbing worries and the adverse effects they can have on your well-being.

Finally, as you re-read or speak your affirmations out loud, it helps if you can *visualise* the ideal outcome in your mind's eye and *feel* the associated emotion. The more you can *see* and *feel* your affirmation, as well as read it or say it out loud, the quicker you'll start to get rid of your worries and bring about the change you desire in your life. So, let's move on to the third step...

STEP 3: CREATE UPBEAT PICTURES IN YOUR MIND

When you're angst-ridden, it's quite likely that as well as being absorbed with the negative self-talk going on inside your head, pictures of your worst nightmare may also be flashing across the screen in your mind, although sometimes they go by so quickly, you may not even notice them.

Pictures, like the words you use in your internal dialogue, are a very powerful way of communicating with your subconscious. And as we've discussed before, whatever you focus on in your conscious mind gets reinforced in your subconscious. So, just as you need to replace doubts and worries by asking the *how can I..?* question or repeating positive affirmations, it's equally important to replace any scary movie that may be going on inside your head with images that reflect your ideal outcome.

And this is where creative visualisation comes in.

Creative visualisation harnesses the power of your imagination to help bring about favourable changes in your life. We all see the things that make up our everyday lives in our mind's eye. If I say to you: *what's your neighbourhood like*? you immediately see a picture of it on the screen in your mind. You don't have to spend time thinking about what your neighbourhood is really like, it's right there in front of you inside your head. This is creative visualisation.

When we're not actively engaged in something that holds our complete attention, our mind wanders off to something else. As this happens, we not only hear dialogue going on inside our head, we literally also see the situation in our mind's eye, as though it were right in front of us. Sometimes, these pictures flash by so quickly we barely notice them, but often they're so vivid and real we can even feel what it's like to be there.

In the same way that you visualise your neighbourhood, you also visualise your troubles and worries. So, just as we've spoken about using affirmations to help get rid of your doubts and worries, it's equally important to create uplifting pictures in your mind's eye to replace any scary images that may be flashing by inside.

The creative visualisation process

The starting point is to identify the aspect of your life that you're worried about and want to deal with more effectively. You may have health problems or are in a personal relationship that isn't working. You may have a crisis of confidence or be worried about an upcoming event. You may have financial concerns or be worried about your personal safety.

Once you've chosen the area you want to work on, create an affirmation that is the polar opposite of the particular worry you have, i.e. it encapsulates what you want rather than what you're worried about. Then create a vivid picture or movie in your mind to reinforce your affirmation. See yourself enjoying what you want and feeling happy and satisfied with it. The more vivid and detailed the picture, the better.

You may want to sit or lie down in a quiet place where you won't be disturbed. It might be at home, seated in your parked car or out in the countryside. The place doesn't have to be totally silent, but if there's background noise, make sure that it doesn't intrude on your thoughts. When you're settled in a comfortable position, close your eyes and focus on your breathing, which should be slow and steady, as this will help you relax and let go of intrusive thoughts. Then say your affirmation and visualise the associated outcome in your mind's eye.

Make sure you use as much imagination as you can muster to paint a clear picture of the outcome you want to create in reality. Think about the location, what you and other people may be saying or doing, whether there are any objects in your movie and their effect. The more detail you can build into your mental picture, the greater the impact on your subconscious. Finally, let go of the picture, trusting that your subconscious will help bring your inner image into reality in your outer world.

This whole process may take just a few minutes, but if you can maintain the picture in your mind for longer, so much the better.

Here are a couple of examples:

If you need to have a difficult conversation with your boss, a demanding co-worker or thoughtless neighbour, you might say: *I am a confident person, everyday my confidence increases to new heights.* Then picture yourself expressing your needs and feelings in a calm, assertive way. Notice how they listen to you before responding respectfully. Be aware of how you listen carefully to what they're saying, asking them to explain anything you're not clear about. See yourself treating the other person courteously as you exchange different points of view. Then visualise yourself discussing ideas with them that lead to an outcome you're happy with.

If you're feeling tired all the time, you might say: *I abound with good health and awaken with new energy every day,* or *I am strong, healthy and energetic.* Then picture yourself getting up in the morning feeling completely refreshed after a good night's sleep. You're raring to go. See yourself walking effortlessly along the pavement and up the steps to your first appointment. Your friends and colleagues comment on how well you look. You're radiating energy, enthusiasm and sheer joy. It's a great day and you're glad to be alive.

Practice makes perfect

It may take a bit of time and practice to master this process, but you can do it, if you're patient with yourself. At first, you may find it difficult to visualise what you want to accomplish in your mind's eye, but the more you practice, the easier it will become, and the more vivid a picture you'll be able to create. To begin with, the pictures may not be very clear, but as time goes on, you'll get better and better at creating the imagery and will just know what details to add to your internal movie. You can always refer back to Chapter 4 to refresh your memory about the sorts of characteristics you can use to create the pictures in your mind.

If you find that no matter how hard you try, you just can't create a picture or movie of what you want inside your head, find a picture in a magazine or online that encapsulates the sentiment and focus on that instead.

There's one other tip I would like to add here. Sometimes, in the course of the day, 'bad news' pictures flash across the screen of your mind, often prompted by something you're doing or thinking about. For instance, you might be driving down the motorway, and 'see' yourself involved in a car crash. Or you might 'see' yourself walking down the stairs and having a fall. The way to deal with this is to immediately replace the 'bad news' image in your conscious mind with something more positive. So instead, you would see yourself arriving home safely and putting the car away in the garage. Or, confidently reaching the bottom of the stairs and walking along the hallway. The key is not to dwell on the negative picture, but to replace it right away with a positive image that represents the ideal outcome.

STEP 4: FEEL THE FEELING

You may recall that your brain and body communicate with each other via powerful electrochemical signals, so they become synchronised: you feel the way you think, and you think the way you feel. What this means from the point of view of smoothing away your worries is that as you switch your internal dialogue and the pictures on the screen in your mind to something more upbeat, you also need to change how you're feeling inside to something more upbeat.

Often, when you change the thoughts in your conscious mind, you start to develop positive feelings and emotions associated with the desired change in your life. These emotions may include a sense of calm, hope, kindness, compassion, courage, confidence, excitement, happiness and so on.

But sometimes you have to work a little bit harder at creating those positive feelings. This is because your emotions, like your thoughts, have got into the habit of feeling worried, down or demoralised. They keep tugging you back to the emotional status quo that's built up over the years. So, as you say your affirmations and visualise your ideal outcome, try to feel how you would feel if your new thoughts – what you really want – were a reality in your life right now.

One way of doing this is to recall a situation in the past where you were calm, confident or happy, etc. and do your best to replicate that feeling.

Another option is to change how you hold and move your body. You may have noticed that your posture, the level of tension in your muscles, facial expressions and eye contact all differ depending on whether you're feeling worried or upbeat. For example:

- If you slow down your breathing and relax your body, especially your facial muscles, jaw, neck and shoulders, you can induce a sense of calm.
- If you stand up tall with an open posture, hold your head high and look ahead, you can activate a feeling of confidence.

- If you pull your shoulders back, look forward and smile or laugh rather than looking sad or dejected, you can change your mood and actually start to feel much happier and more positive on the inside.

Here are a couple of examples.

Perhaps there's something in your life that's led you to think: *I can't do it.* Maybe it's undertaking a task you've not done before, applying for a change of job, or travelling to a far-flung country. The first step might be to say to yourself in a quietly confident voice: *I can do it,* and then picture the successful outcome as clearly as you can in your mind's eye. As you do so, stand up tall, hold your head high and look straight ahead. Feel yourself calmly and confidently taking the first step. If it helps, think of another situation where you stepped bravely up to the plate and try to replicate that feeling. Then feel a glow of satisfaction as if you had already completed the challenging task.

Maybe you feel as though you're being pulled in different directions or have been pushed to the limit by the pressure of work. Start by saying to yourself in a calm and gentle voice: *I am calm and relaxed in all situations,* then picture yourself dealing with the problems you're facing in a calm and collected way. Take a few moments to let go of the tension in your face, jaw, neck and shoulders, and feel your body relax. Then feel a sense of calm envelope you. If you're having difficulty connecting with these feelings, think of another situation where you felt completely at peace and try to replicate that emotion. And finally, experience a glow of warmth inside, as you see yourself dealing calmly and favourably with all those pressing matters.

The important point here is that you can change how you feel emotionally by changing the way you hold and move your body. This is vital, because you can't think one way and feel another and expect to ease the worries out of your life. You may have heard some people say that affirmations don't work, and they certainly won't work if you're thinking one thing and feeling the complete opposite. Your mind and body have to be synchronised and working in the same direction. The more your mind and body work together in an upbeat fashion, the more you start to undo your worry habits and replace them with something more constructive. Effectively, you're gradually rewiring your brain to work in a more constructive way on an ongoing basis.

Another aspect of 'feel the feeling' is that it is the strength of your emotion that helps draw solutions to the problems you're facing into your life. When you ask the *how can I...?* question, you're giving your subconscious a very clear instruction about what's needed. But this alone is not enough. It is the degree of trust that an answer will be provided, together with the depth of feeling depicting the ideal outcome that actually draws the solution into your life.

STEP 5: TAKE ACTION!

The final step in easing the worries out of your life is to take action. Not only are your thoughts and feelings connected, but so too are your thoughts, feelings and behaviour, i.e. they are part of a cybernetic loop, whereby a change in any one of them creates a change in the other two.

By switching your internal dialogue, pictures and tone of voice from what you don't want to what you *do want*, and by feeling the associated feeling, you're motivated to take action to sort out the problems you're facing. And when this happens, you start to see real, positive change manifest itself in your external life, leading to more favourable outcomes.

This isn't make-believe; it's a reflection and manifestation of the natural laws of the universe. The more you focus on what you want rather than on your worries, and the more you start thinking and feeling in terms of what you can do rather than what you can't do, you set up a force field of energy that motivates you to resolve the difficulties you're facing. This then moves you in the direction you want to go rather than holding you back with doubts and concerns.

By thinking and feeling differently, you become aware of all sorts of choices you didn't notice before, and you start to realise you have skills and qualities you didn't think you had. As a result, your worries no longer weigh you down or hold you back. You're motivated to behave differently, and this leads to more positive outcomes in your life. But the important thing here is you need to *take action*, and I can't emphasise this enough. It's not sufficient to say your affirmations and visualise, and then sit back and wait for all your problems to somehow be magically solved. It's taking the action that ultimately makes all the difference in your external life.

There's another tip I would like to share with you, which is also worth trying. Sometimes you don't feel like doing something you need to do, and you're tempted not to do it. But if you say: *right, I'm going to do it* and you take action, what invariably happens is that it's not as bad as you thought it was going to be. You even start to feel like doing what you initially didn't want to do, and your thoughts become more positive! This is just another example of the cybernetic loop at work.

A FEW HINTS

Don't try to be a perfectionist. If your mind wanders off and starts dwelling on something else as you go through this step-by-step process, just bring your thoughts gently back to the new affirmation you want to instil in your mind. And if you can't visualise the perfect picture in your mind's eye or feel great depth of feeling to support your affirmation and imagery, so be it. Just follow the process as best you can. And don't be tempted to give up.

You can't expect to change the way you think and feel about the problems you're facing by just deciding to do it. That's a very important starting point, but it takes a bit of time and practice to change old thinking and feeling habits. So, do your best to keep your thoughts and emotions focused on your ideal outcome and off your doubts and fears. You'll find it gets easier as you gain a bit of momentum.

And don't be tempted to think none of this is working. Just trust the process. At first, you might not notice much difference, but gradually you'll find that your troubles and worries have less of a hold on you. Then, with a bit more practice, you'll notice you can deal with them more effectively. And as you master these techniques even more, you'll find you just get on and do whatever needs to be done without being immobilised by your doubts and fears. At that point, mind numbing worries will have become a thing of the past.

I know this can be hard to begin with, but you'll make it through if you stay with it. I found it difficult at first, but just kept going until it all came together. Change isn't always easy, so be patient with yourself. You really can transform the way you deal with the problems in your life. It may take a bit of time to perfect this step-by-step approach, but as a former 5-star worrier, I can vouch for the fact that it works if you gently persist. And it certainly beats experiencing day after day of draining worry that never goes away.

PUTTING IT ALL INTO PRACTICE

Ten years ago, my ability to handle stress and worry were really put to the test. My mum and dad were involved in a head-on collision when they were hit by a car being driven on the wrong side of the road. They were both hospitalised and although they came through the crash, their health started to deteriorate. Over the next five years, my dad developed a serious heart condition and experienced dementia before passing away, while my mum had a series of major strokes before following him a year later.

At the time, I was running my own market research business, but I stopped working to provide support, partly because I thought the world of them, and partly because there was no-one else who could help.

It was heart-breaking to see them go downhill and suffer so much, something I couldn't do anything about. On top of that, there were endless challenges in dealing with the health authorities and finding suitable care for them.

A lot of things were totally beyond my control, but I resolved I'd focus on what I could control to make a difference for them… and for me. In those moments of intense pressure and heartache, I would say to myself: *I am calm and relaxed in all situations,* and would visualise myself calmly doing whatever needed to be done next…whether driving to the hospital, sitting quietly by my mum's bedside or discussing her prognosis with the doctors.

And when I didn't know what to do for the best, I would ask: *how can I improve things*? Or *what can I do to help*? And there was always an answer. I couldn't solve her health problems – or my dad's before her – but I could make sure that they had not only the right sort of care, but kind and compassionate care. I could provide moral support. I could speak with the doctors. I could make phone calls and look after the myriad of practical things that needed sorting out.

It was a heart-breaking time, but what I'd learnt many years before – what I've spoken about in this book – held me in good stead and saw me through. So, keep in mind that whatever's happening out there, we each have control over our thoughts, feelings and behaviour, which means we have a choice over how we deal with our troubles and worries.

KEY POINTS

1. The step-by-step process for overcoming worry includes the following five steps:
   (i) recognise the signs of worry;
   (ii) take control of your internal dialogue and the tone of voice you use;
   (iii) create upbeat pictures in your mind;
   (iv) feel the feeling; and
   (v) take action!
2. The tell-tale signs that you're preoccupied with your troubles and worries include coming out with a lot of negative words when speaking to yourself, using an anxious tone of voice, seeing 'bad news' pictures flash across the screen in your mind, feeling tightness or tension in your body, feeling down emotionally, and delaying or avoiding action that might otherwise be helpful.
3. There are three techniques you can use to develop positive internal dialogue:
   (i) ask yourself the *how can I...?* question;
   (ii) use vocabulary that focuses on your ideal outcome; and
   (iii) devise an appropriate affirmation and repeat it to yourself.

4. Affirmations must be personal (i.e. include the words ‘I’ or ‘my’), focus on your ideal outcome and be in the present tense.
5. Creative visualisation can be used to harness the power of your imagination in order to bring about favourable changes in your life.
6. Affirmations and creative visualisation should be used as often as possible during the course of the day, especially when you notice that your thoughts are focused on your troubles and worries.
7. As you focus your conscious mind on what you want, you start to develop positive emotions associated with the desired change in your life. You can also change how you feel emotionally by altering your posture, facial expressions and level of tension in your face and body.
8. You can’t think one way and feel another and expect to ease the worries out of your life. Your mind and body have to be synchronised and working in the same direction.
9. The more you start thinking and feeling in terms of what you can do rather than what you can’t, you set up a force field of energy that motivates you to take action, with the result that you begin to see positive change and more favourable outcomes manifest themselves in your external life.

QUESTIONS

Start by selecting one of the worries that you identified after reading Chapter 4, and then complete the statements outlined below. The purpose of this exercise is to help you put the 5-step process into practice, so you can initiate positive change in the way you think and feel about your worries, as well as the actions you subsequently take. Think about each statement and write (or type) out all the ideas that come into your mind. What you're looking for is a new, more effective way of dealing with the worry you have selected.

1. I use the following affirmation to switch my internal dialogue from what I don't want (my worry) to what I do want (my ideal outcome)...
2. The tone of voice I use when I repeat my affirmation is…
3. This is a description of the creative visualisation I use to picture what I want…
4. My affirmation and visualisation encourage me to feel… (Record how you will feel emotionally when you've got rid of your worry and accomplished what you want, and do your best to feel those feelings).
5. In order to feel the way I want to feel, I make the following changes to my posture, facial expressions and level of tension in my face and body…
6. The actions I'm motivated to take to sort out my worry and accomplish what I want are… (If you get stuck on this one, ask yourself: *How can I...?)*

Before wrapping up this chapter, there is something else I'd like to add, which will make all the difference in terms of easing the worries out of your life, and it's this…

If you read this book to simply learn about how worry manifests itself in your life and what to do about it in **theory**, it won't transform your life. It's important to complete the exercises at the end of each chapter, and then actually **apply** the ideas you've come up with in your everyday life. It goes without saying that you need to learn how to deal with worry in order to get rid of it, but the real change and the real benefits come when you put the learnings into practice.

PART 3:
APPLYING THE
5-STEP PROCESS

CHAPTER 6:
LETTING GO OF THE PAST

THE PAST DOES NOT DICTATE THE FUTURE

What I'd like to do in the remaining chapters is show how you can take the 5-step process and apply it in specific situations that cause stress and worry, so you can get relief from your concerns and find some peace of mind.

So, let's start with letting go of the past, which is eminently possible, irrespective of your genetic make-up, your upbringing and the experiences you've been through. Just because something didn't go right before doesn't mean to say it won't go right in the future. If you can let go of the past, it opens up all sorts of possibilities.

When we dwell on the past, it's typically for one of three reasons. It may be because we feel wronged in some way, because of something that happened to us. Alternatively, we may be overcome with regret, because of something we said or did, which we feel we shouldn't have done. And finally, we may dwell on the past as a result of a loss, which causes great sorrow or grief. (I'm going to talk more about these first two scenarios in Chapters 7 and 8, but I'm not going to cover how to cope with grief, because that's a special case, which is beyond the scope of this book.)

If you feel you've been wronged, either when you were growing up or as an adult, it's very easy – and understandable – to become totally preoccupied with the injustice of it all. You can spend hours replaying what happened in your mind, going over every detail again and again. Maybe you're trying to understand what motivated someone to behave in the way they did. Why was it that they said or did something so hurtful? Perhaps you can't stand the unfairness of it all. Or maybe you feel that if you go over it just one more time, it will somehow not seem as bad or will make more sense.

Then there are those times when you dwell on the past because of something you said or did which you deeply regret; we've all done this at some time or another. Perhaps you made a mistake that affected those around you, or which led to a bad outcome from your own point of view. Maybe you acted in a way that caused a long-held dream to die. Then, racked with guilt, you go over what you feel you *should* or *could* have said and done. You beat yourself up time and time again.

Whether you feel wronged because of something that happened to you in the past, or are beside yourself with remorse because of something you said or did, you can't actually change what's gone before, no matter how much you might want to.

Every time you replay a hurtful incident in your mind, you reinforce all the negative thoughts and feelings, which can be very painful. You only make matters worse by continually going over it all. What's more, these painful thoughts and feelings sap your energy and immobilise you. You get stuck in the past and find it difficult to move on. You can't make the most of the present moment and enjoy your life to the full. And you run the real risk of letting countless opportunities pass you by.

So, you must let go of the past.

If you're tempted to say you can't do that, because you've been so badly hurt, I would simply say think again. I don't know what's happened to you or how badly you've been hurt. But I do know the universe in all its guises will come to your aid and help you move on if you seek its help. If you give it a chance, new doors will open in ways you can't imagine right now.

Alternatively, if you're someone who thinks you don't deserve to move on because of something you said or did, you need to reconsider. Life will always give you another chance. There's not a single person walking this planet who has led a perfect life. We have all said and done things we regret and that fill us with remorse. Why deny the rest of the world the benefit of all your qualities and talents simply because you did something wrong in the past? And why deny yourself the satisfaction and fulfilment of making a contribution in a way that only you can, because you're you? So, don't ruminate over past mistakes or let them eat away inside you. Instead focus your thoughts on what you can do right now to start realising your full potential.

You're not a victim of your past.

You have a choice: you can stay trapped in what's gone before or you can focus on making your life better today and in the future, irrespective of what's happened. Keep in mind you're the person you are today, partly because of your upbringing and past experiences. While some of the things that happened may have been very hurtful and upsetting, it's possible to learn from these experiences and even benefit from them. And if you choose, you can also help other people who are going through what you've been through.

But there's one very important point I need to make here. Sometimes there are those terrible experiences involving trauma or abuse that are very difficult to leave behind, no matter how hard you try. If this applies to you, I recommend you seek help from a qualified medical professional – if you haven't already done so – in order to help deal with what happened. This book is not intended to replace qualified medical support.

With that said, let's move on to the art of letting go of the past.

STEP 1: ACKNOWLEDGE YOU'RE CAUGHT IN THE PAST AND ACCEPT WHAT HAPPENED

The starting point in letting go is to be honest with yourself and *acknowledge* you're caught in the past. Don't be tempted to try and pretend you're not affected by what's gone before, because this is self-defeating and only perpetuates the problem. Unresolved past experiences can have all sorts of negative effects that impact how you deal with life's difficulties, how well you get on with other people and what you accomplish, which in turn affect your happiness and well-being. In order to move on, you need to acknowledge what's happened, so you can deal with the after-effects once and for all.

Having acknowledged you're caught in the past, it's also important to *accept* what happened. Sadly, you can't rewrite history and change what's gone before, but you can change how you view what happened…and the subsequent effect it may be having on you. And just to be absolutely clear, this isn't about pretending that something upsetting didn't happen, it's about accepting you can't undo what's already occurred, but you can learn from the experience and change how you respond going forward.

So, if you feel you've been wronged in some way or you're tempted to engage in 'if only' thinking, (e.g. *if only I hadn't been laid off, if only I hadn't messed up,* or *things would be different if my partner hadn't walked out*), there are probably some unhelpful thoughts you need to get rid of. This sort of thinking only makes the angst far worse, so for your own sake and the sake of those close to you, you need to replace it with something more constructive.

All the heartache you experience in the present actually comes from how you **continue to think and feel** about the past experience **now**, not the past experience itself. This is sometimes very hard to accept when you've been wronged or feel badly hurt, but the more you hang on to the angst about what's gone before, the more entrenched and unable to move on you become.

You need to be willing to accept – really accept – that you can't change what's already happened, so there's no point in continuing to rail against it by going over it all again and again. But what you can change is how you think and feel about it now, and the actions you decide to take in the present. And the really uplifting thing is that when you do this, you get some respite from all the anguish, and open the door to some happiness and peace of mind.

STEP 2: TAKE CONTROL OF YOUR INTERNAL DIALOGUE AND THE TONE OF VOICE YOU USE

When you're feeling constantly overwhelmed by a bad experience, it's difficult to imagine how you could ever be free of all the draining thoughts and uncomfortable feelings it brings up, but you can.

You'll recall that our subconscious takes its cues from our conscious mind. The more we focus our mind on negative self-talk – *if only it hadn't happened, it wasn't fair, things could have been different,* and so on – the more we reinforce negative emotions inside us, and the worse we feel. Conversely, if we switch our internal dialogue to something more constructive, we start to induce some calm and peace of mind.

The minute you notice you're dwelling on something negative that happened in the past, you can do one of two things (or ideally both):

1. Your first option is to ask yourself: *how can I let go of the past?* Or *how can I move on from what's happened*? This has the effect of firing up your subconscious to help find a way forward.
2. Secondly, you can replace your distressing thoughts with a calming affirmation that resonates with you. This breaks your

train of thought and switches your focus from the negativity of the past to the possibilities of the future. So, if angst about the past takes hold, try replacing those thoughts with something like:

I live happily in the here and now
I am at peace and ready to move on
I allow peace and harmony to flow into my life
I clear the way so I can lead a free, responsible life
I am free to move forward in my life
I am on the path to a brighter future
I am free to live the life of my dreams

These affirmations can be applied in a variety of different circumstances, but if you'd rather devise an affirmation of your own, particularly if you want something more specific, that's great, just remember it needs to be personal, in the present tense and focusing on your ideal outcome. You can refer back to Chapter 5 if you want to refresh your memory about how to create an affirmation.

Do your best to say your affirmation with a tone of voice that reflects its sentiment, whether it be a sense of calm, inner peace, enthusiasm or excitement. Keep in mind that it's no good just saying your affirmation once or twice. You need to repeat it as often as you can, and especially when you find yourself dwelling on something negative from the past.

STEP 3: CREATE UPBEAT PICTURES IN YOUR MIND OF A NEW FUTURE

You also need to picture yourself feeling calm and looking forward to a brighter future, which isn't always easy when you're feeling wound up. So, if you're having difficulty visualising this in your mind's eye, look at some serene images and listen to some soothing music, both of which can help induce a sense of calm. The great thing about today's technology is that it allows you to have photographs, video and music with you at all times on your tablet, iPhone or iPod, so make full use of these devices.

Often bad memories make themselves known in your mind through vivid imagery or distressing sounds, like someone shouting at you. Together, they can induce all sorts of negative feelings, such as fear, anger, resentment, sadness, guilt, shame or lack of confidence. So, it's really important to start noticing not only the angst-ridden dialogue going on inside your head, but also any pictures or sounds that reinforce the negative self-talk. If something upsetting crosses your radar, the key is to switch your focus to an image that's calming or uplifting.

STEP 4: FEEL THE FEELING

The more you can change the negative self-talk and pictures, the more you'll induce positive emotions and won't feel so bad. And when you don't feel so bad, you start to realise you don't have to be held back by the past. You have a choice. And when you realise you have a choice, you're motivated to find a new, happier way forward.

That being said, I'm not going to pretend this transition will happen overnight, because like us all, your old way of thinking and feeling has become a habit. One of the challenges in trying to move on is that your thoughts and feelings are often pulling in different directions. You may be saying your affirmations and creating upbeat images in your mind, and yet it seems incredibly difficult to shake off anxious or angry feelings that originate from the past.

If this applies to you, keep in mind that you can change your emotional state by changing how you hold and move your body to reflect the way you want to feel. If you feel angry and find that your jaw is clenched, your facial muscles are tight and your body muscles are tense, consciously relax your body and slow your breathing down; this will help induce a sense of calm. If you feel dejected and demotivated, look up, pull your shoulders back and smile; this will lift your spirits. You really can change how you feel by changing your posture and the way you move.

UNDERSTANDING WHY

One of the things we often do when dwelling on the past is try and understand why people did what they did or how certain events came about. Gaining an understanding of why and how can be immensely helpful in coming to terms with what happened, so we can move on and leave all the unhappiness behind us. But sometimes it's not possible to find out why someone behaved the way they did, or how a situation actually unfolded. This may be because the people involved are no longer around, or if they are, they're unwilling or unable to explain.

When you go over something again and again, trying to rationalise what happened, you become so emotionally involved that the whole process makes you feel even worse. What's more, because you don't have all the information you need to reach an answer, there's a risk of making inaccurate assumptions and settling on the worst possible explanation, which may or may not apply. Sometimes, the real explanation is something you would never even have dreamed of.

Just as you can't rewrite history, if you can't establish why or how something happened, then – as difficult as it may be – you need to accept this as well. Repeatedly going over the same thing, trying to make sense of it all when no explanation can readily be found, only keeps you stuck in the past and unable to move on.

If you find yourself in this situation, try switching your thoughts to a positive affirmation that resonates with you, and picture in your mind's eye – or focus outwardly on – some serene images, while listening to some soothing music.

STEP 5: CHANGE THE WAY YOU BEHAVE

Past experiences provide a valuable opportunity to learn from what happened, even if they were very upsetting. So, it's important to consider what took place and be clear about how it affected your actions at the time. You can then stand back and reflect on what you've learnt and what you can do differently in the future.

Once you've decided what steps to take, be sure to take action right away so you create some momentum that will lead to more positive outcomes in your life. It's very tempting to make plans and then not implement them, because old habits get in the way, so take action as soon as possible. What you decide to do differently will depend on what occurred in the past, how it affected you, what you've learnt and how it's empowered you going forward, but you may want to consider the following sorts of actions:

In order to move on, it helps enormously if you can express your thoughts and feelings rather than keeping them bottled up inside. Consider speaking to a trusted friend or family member about what happened, how it affected you then and how it continues to affect you now. Doing this often helps you sort out what needs to be done so you can leave the past behind. But if, for whatever reason, you're not able to talk to someone about what happened, write everything down in a journal. This can clarify things in your own mind and help you decide what to do next.

You may then decide to speak with or write to the person who has hurt you – if that's possible – but before you do so, consider whether it's a wise thing to do. If there's a risk of opening old wounds or being hurt further, you may want to reconsider whether this really is the best course of action. Also, if it's someone you care about, you may want to give thought to the impact on them of raising the matter.

If you do decide to go ahead and speak with the person concerned, approach the discussion with the intention of expressing your thoughts and feelings so you can move on from what happened. This gives the other person an opportunity to explain why they did what they did, which may (although not necessarily) help you come to terms with what happened. It may also lead to a discussion between the two of you about how things can be handled differently in the future, or at the other extreme, you may decide to minimise contact with that person or even walk away altogether. There are many possible outcomes. Trust your intuition about what to do. But most importantly of all, don't engage in the discussion simply to make the other person feel bad and to emphasise how awful it's been and continues to be for you. By all means express your thoughts and feelings, but let it be with the intention of finding a better way forward rather than perpetuating all the hurt or anger.

If it's not possible to speak with the person who has hurt you, because they're not prepared to speak with you, they've passed away or you no longer have contact with them, then consider writing a letter expressing your thoughts and feelings, again with the intention of being able to move on. This whole process can be very cathartic. Whether or not you actually send the letter will depend on the circumstances, but in a way that doesn't matter, because the purpose of writing it is to free yourself from the past. If you don't send the letter, then destroy it; don't keep rereading it, because the letter marks a watershed; a time when you move on from the past to a better future.

If the reason you're caught up in the past is because of something you said or did that you now regret, you may want to consider apologising to the person concerned, if you've not already done so. You can either speak with them – if that's possible – or write a letter in the way described above. Let it be a sincere apology, and one that's intended to help you both move on from what happened. If you can redress what you did then offer to do so, but be prepared for the possibility that the person concerned may – or may not – accept your apology or be willing to move forward in the way you would like. Whatever the outcome, you will then have done all you can do, and it's time to leave the mistake behind you.

Next, there may be situations you now avoid because of a bad experience in the past. Perhaps you won't confront a family member's unreasonable behaviour for fear of being rebuffed. Or maybe you said something naïve to your colleagues and now won't speak up in meetings for fear of making a fool of yourself. Or perhaps you were bitten by a dog, so always cross the street when you see one coming towards you. As hard as it may sound, the best way to overcome these fears and move on is to do the very thing you fear. As they say in India: *look the tiger in the eye*. Take one tiny step at a time, and as you do, the hold your fear has on you will gradually diminish and becomes more manageable.

Finally, there may be specific actions you can take that you would not have taken in the past. You may decide to move to a new area, spend more time with your family, change your job, take up a new hobby, hire a personal trainer, branch out on your own, and so on. Whatever the action, let it be something that moves your life forward rather than holding you back.

GUIDED IMAGERY

If, in spite of your best efforts to implement the 5-step process, you're still finding it hard to let go of something hurtful or unpleasant that happened in the past, I suggest trying the guided imagery outlined below.

Start by sitting or lying down in a comfortable position in a quiet place where you won't be disturbed. It might be at home, in your office or seated in your parked car. The place doesn't have to be totally silent, but if there is background noise, make sure it doesn't intrude on your thoughts. Close your eyes and, for a few minutes, focus on your breathing, which should be slow and steady, as this will help you to relax.

Then imagine yourself in a peaceful setting, sitting quietly beside a stream that flows gently by. It's a balmy summer afternoon; the sun is shining; you feel its warmth; the sky is blue; a light breeze rustles the leaves in the trees and the birds are singing a little way off. You hear the soothing sound of the water; the light flickers on the surface of the stream and a few leaves float quietly by.

Bring your attention to the thoughts you want to release. Place them very gently on the surface of the stream and let them go like the leaves you noticed earlier. Follow them as they float slowly away, becoming smaller and smaller, and less significant with each passing moment until they're out of sight. They've gone, dissolved into the water, gone back to nothing. A stillness and calm envelopes your whole being. You feel at peace with yourself, the world and those around you.

This imagery is not intended to replace the 5-step process; it's supplementary, another technique to help you let go of the past. Feel free to embellish it further so that it really resonates with you, but the key is gently placing those worrying thoughts about the past on the surface of the stream and letting them go.

MOVING ON

It's not always easy to make peace with what has gone before, and move on, particularly if you've been deeply hurt, but you can do it. Just be patient with yourself; take it slowly, and don't be tempted to give up.

I remember when a former boyfriend of mine told me that he wanted to end our relationship, because an old flame had reappeared in his life. It stopped me in my tracks. Everything had seemed to be going so well, and then in a moment, it was over. In the weeks and months that followed, I gradually got used to the idea. It wasn't his fault – or hers – it was just the way it was. But while I clung on to what had been, I was shutting down my life. In the words of Alexander Graham Bell: *we often look so long and so regretfully upon the closed door that we do not see the one which has opened for us.*

So, in your own life, don't look long and regretfully at the closed door. Each time you find yourself dwelling on unhappy memories, gently switch your thoughts to a calming or uplifting affirmation. Visualise a happier future. Try the guided imagery. And little by little, your horizons will expand and a new door will open. And when it does, be sure to take action.

KEY POINTS

1. Whether you feel wronged because of something that happened to you in the past, or are beside yourself with remorse because of something you said or did, you can't actually change what's gone before, no matter how much you might want to.
2. Every time you replay a hurtful incident in your mind, you reinforce all the negative thoughts and feelings. This is not only

painful, but it also saps your energy and immobilises you. As a result, you get stuck and find it hard to move on.

3. Although it may seem hard to believe, you have a choice: you can stay trapped in what's gone before or you can focus on making your life better today and in the future.

4. The first step is to acknowledge you're caught in the past and accept what's happened.

5. All the heartache you experience in the present actually comes from how you continue to think and feel about the past experience now, not the past experience itself. So, the second step is to take control of your internal dialogue by using a calming or uplifting affirmation and asking: *how can I move on*? Next, create upbeat pictures in your mind of a bright new future.

6. You can help change your emotional state by altering how you move and hold your body to reflect the way you want to feel.

7. Past experiences provide a valuable opportunity to learn from what happened, and help identify what you can do differently in the future. Once you've decided, you need to take action right away, because it can be tempting to make plans and then not implement them, as old habits get in the way.

8. Guided imagery can be used to help let go of hurtful and unpleasant things from the past.

9. It's not always easy to make peace with what has gone before, and move on, particularly if you've been deeply hurt, but you can do it. Just be patient with yourself, and take it slowly.

10. There's one important caveat to all of this: if you've experienced trauma or abuse that you find difficult to leave behind, seek help from a qualified medical professional in order to deal with what happened. This book is not intended to replace qualified medical support, particularly if you have an anxiety disorder.

QUESTIONS

If you're having difficulty moving on from something that happened in the past, I suggest completing the following exercise, which is designed to help you learn from the experience, and change the way you think, feel and behave so you can move forward in your life.

The exercise consists of two parts:

- Seven questions to help clarify how the past experience is affecting you now and what you can learn from it, and
- Seven sentences for you to complete to help you move forward in your life.

Think carefully about each of the questions and see what thoughts float to the surface. Then write (or type) out all the ideas that come into your conscious mind, remembering there are no right or wrong answers. This process can help find ways of moving on that you might not otherwise have thought of.

Past Experience

1. What really happened?
2. Why did it happen? (If you know the answer.)
3. How did the experience affect your thoughts, feelings and behaviour at the time?
4. And how is the experience affecting your thoughts, feelings and behaviour now?
5. What sort of physical reactions occur in your body when you think about what happened?
6. How is the experience affecting your outlook and what you believe you can accomplish?

7. What can you learn from the experience that will help you move on? (Consider what good has come out of your experience and what you can do differently going forward).

When considering your thoughts, try to include not only your internal dialogue, but also the tone of voice you use and any pictures that may flash across the screen in your mind.

Moving On

1. I use the following affirmation to help me let go of the past and move on in my life…
2. The tone of voice I use when I repeat my affirmation is…
3. This is a description of the creative visualisation I use to help me move on in my life…
4. My affirmation and visualisation encourage me to feel… (Record how you will feel emotionally when you've let go of the past and moved on, and do your best to feel those feelings.)
5. In order to feel the way I want to feel, I make the following changes to my posture, facial expressions and level of tension in my face and body…
6. I listen to the following piece of music (or video) to reinforce my affirmation, visualisation and feelings…
7. The actions I'm motivated to take to let go of the past and move on are… (If you get stuck on this one, refer back to what you have learnt, and ask yourself: *how can I move on*?)

CHAPTER 7: PUTTING AN END TO BLAME AND RESENTMENT

In the previous chapter, we looked at why it's important to put the past behind us, together with the 5-step process for letting go of what's gone before. Building on that foundation, I would now like to take a closer look at two special cases, namely putting an end to blame and resentment.

Although blame and resentment sometimes go hand-in-hand, they're actually different concepts. Blame refers to censuring someone perceived to be responsible for something that has gone wrong, whereas resentment is holding on to a grievance that originates from having been badly treated in one way or another.

THE BLAME GAME

When something goes wrong, or doesn't work out as we might have hoped, all of us have a deep-seated need to explain what happened and why. Typically, this leads to one of three responses:

1. There are people who are quick to point the finger at someone else and deny any part they may have played in the situation themselves.
2. Then there are those who take on the full burden of responsibility themselves, believing that they – and they alone – are to blame for what happened. (This will be covered in the next chapter in the context of letting go of guilt.)

3. And finally, there are those who are not interested in apportioning blame. Instead, they just want to understand what happened and why, so the situation can be resolved, and they can learn how to avoid something similar happening in the future.

The last of these responses is by far the most effective in everyday life, but first, let's take a look at what happens when we start blaming other people.

BLAMING OTHERS

When something goes wrong, we can all be tempted to point the finger at someone or something else, whether it's a demanding parent when we were growing up, an uncaring spouse, a thoughtless friend, an unreasonable boss, the government or the economy. On the face of it, blaming others absolves us of all responsibility. If something or someone else is to blame, then we can say: *it's not my fault, I couldn't help it, I had no choice,* and other such thoughts.

It may be that we are indeed totally blameless and are not responsible for the misfortune that occurred. On the other hand, we may bear some responsibility for what was said and done, and the choices made. Obviously, it's better if we can be totally honest with ourselves about what really happened so we can learn from the experience, respond more positively and avoid similar situations in the future.

But the point I'd like to emphasise here is that, regardless of who is responsible and to what extent, we are not doing ourselves any favours by blaming others for what happened. The minute we do that, we take on the mantle of a victim, someone who has no choice but to accept the outcome. And this is when things start to go downhill.

When we feel we have no control over a situation, and are unable to influence what's happening in any way, we get stuck and find it difficult to move on. When we think we can't change things for the better, our negative thoughts lead to feelings of despondency and helplessness, which demotivate us even more. This in turn can lead to great unhappiness, frustration and disappointment. So, in the interests of our mental and emotional well-being, it's essential to avoid the blame game.

PUTTING AN END TO BLAME

If something goes wrong, or doesn't work out as you might have hoped, rather than blaming someone else for what happened, you need to adopt a different approach; one that concentrates on learning from the experience, exploring what can be done to improve the situation and recognising what can be done differently in the future.

This is fundamentally different from the blame game, because it switches the focus from finding fault and conveying recriminations to identifying what can be done right now to improve things and avoid something similar happening in the future. This switch effectively changes the way you think and feel about what happened, as well as how you subsequently behave. You can't change what's gone before, but you can change how you're going to respond going forward, and this realisation can be remarkably empowering.

Be clear about what happened and why

The starting point is to be clear about what has caused you to blame someone else for what occurred, which involves looking at exactly *what happened*, and *why*. Do your best to view the situation as objectively as you can without fuelling any anger or anxiety you might be feeling.

As well as considering what happened *outside* of you – the incident, if you like – it's also important to consider what's going on *inside*. So, move on to ask: *what are your thoughts about it all?* Remember, this includes not only what you're saying to yourself, but also the tone of voice you're using and any pictures that are flashing across the screen in your mind's eye. And, *how does it make you feel*? Perhaps the incident reminds you of something similar that happened in the past, which only adds fuel to your emotions.

And you need to explore *what actions you have taken in response, and why*. The important thing here is to get clear in your mind the part you played, how it has affected you and how it continues to affect you.

The answers to these questions can provide enormous insight in terms of getting a better understanding of everything's that happened, as well as helping decide if there is any remedial action you can take right now, and how you can respond differently in the future.

You may find that asking yourself the *what* and *why* questions helps transform how you think and feel about everything. Rather than feeling angry or upset if you consider someone else is to blame, you start to feel hopeful, and that maybe things aren't as bad as you thought. And when this happens, you're motivated to behave more positively and move forward in your life.

Switch from blaming to calming thoughts and feelings

But if you notice that your thoughts keep drifting back to blaming, gently switch those thoughts to something more calming. I know this isn't easy, particularly if you feel angry about what's happened, but if you persist, you'll gradually find that your conscious mind can let go of the accusatory thoughts. Try using one of the affirmations detailed in Chapter 6, or devise one of your own. The key is to choose a statement that really resonates with you so that it has heartfelt impact, and changes the way you think and feel.

As you say the affirmation to yourself in a relaxed tone of voice, try to visualise a calming image in your mind's eye, and sense yourself feeling at peace inside. To help synchronise your thoughts and feelings, consciously relax the muscles in your face and body, and slow your breathing down.

Take action

The final step in moving on from the blame game is to take action. If you've been blaming someone else for something that's happened in your life, consider speaking or writing to the person concerned to see what can be done to resolve the situation. If this is not feasible or appropriate for whatever reason, then ask yourself: *what can I do right now to improve things?* Or *how can I move on?* The answer may be obvious from the questions you posed earlier in this process, but if not, asking the *how can I...?* question sets up a force field of energy that attracts ideas and possible solutions into your life. Remember, your subconscious is incredibly resourceful, its efforts just need to be channelled in the right direction. Trust that it will come up with the perfect answer for you.

The problem with the blame game is that it keeps you stuck where you are, and reduces your ability to take some form of action and move on. But the situation is what it is, so focus on how you can improve things and do your best to find a way forward rather than concentrating on the cause of your anger and continuing to apportion blame.

THE DOWNSIDE OF RESENTMENT

Resentment is all about replaying – over and over again – in our mind an incident that's hurt or angered us, while at the same time reliving all the associated feelings that can fuel our outrage, exasperation and bitterness. In short, resentment is not conducive to happiness and peace of mind.

One of its most destructive aspects is that we simply can't let go of the resentful thoughts. They're with us when we get up in the morning, when we get in the car and when we stop for lunch. They interfere with our work, detract from our pleasure, and won't let go when we put our head on the pillow at night. They're there all the time. We replay everything in the minutest detail inside our head, and in doing so, get more and more agitated about what's happened.

Resentment can be triggered by one of two things:

1. Someone we know – a partner, family member, friend, colleague, someone in a position of authority or the government – may *say* or *do* something that we consider to be hurtful, disrespectful or in some way unacceptable.
2. Resentment can also be triggered if we believe that someone has *not done* all that we feel they *should have done* for us. This is obviously very subjective and can vary enormously from person to person, and situation to situation.

Another thing to keep in mind is that the part played by the other person may – or may not – have been intentional. Their behaviour may have been deliberately hurtful, disrespectful or uncaring, or they may have said or done something quite unwittingly, without really thinking. Whatever the motivation, it's important to deal with any resentment we may be harbouring, otherwise it can undermine the relationship with the person concerned and also have a knock-on effect in other areas of our lives.

On the face of it, resentment is triggered by a one-off incident, but more often than not, it's a repeat episode of something that's happened many times before. And it's the history that sends us up the wall and across the ceiling. Before we know where we are, we're going over everything again and again, reliving the lack of consideration and unacceptability of it all.

So, why do we keep rehashing these hurtful episodes from our past when all they're doing is dragging us down?

As mentioned before, it's part of human nature to mentally revisit upsetting experiences as a way of processing and coming to terms with what happened. But, and it's a very important but, this thought process needs to be constructive rather than destructive, i.e. it needs to help us move on rather than keeping us stuck in the past.

Typically, what happens when going over everything again is that we believe we'll somehow gain the justice we think we're owed. What we're doing is hanging on to the need to be right, which can stop us from letting go of the hurt and anger, and finding some peace of mind. I'm reminded of that much quoted question: *would you rather be happy or would you rather be right*? Each of us has to decide, and as passionate as I am about fairness, when it comes to revisiting old wounds, I would rather move on and find some happiness and inner peace.

And another important point: if there's any temptation to get even, please keep in mind that revenge is not sweet; it does not lead to fulfilment or peace of mind. We achieve nothing by trying to get even with the other person, or proving we're right and they're wrong. In fact, they may be enjoying life and not be in the least bit troubled by the issues we keep turning over in our minds. If we continue to harbour resentment, it hurts us far more than the person towards whom we bear a grudge. We simply can't move on mentally and emotionally, while we're in that frame of mind.

LETTING GO OF RESENTMENT

Becoming more aware

If resentment is an issue in your life, the first step in letting go is to become aware of when you keep churning over old grievances in your mind, reliving all the hurt and anger. Sometimes, there's a tendency to try and ignore these troublesome thoughts, fight your way through them or pretend they don't matter. But this is nothing more than denial and isn't going to get you anywhere. You need to be honest with yourself.

Another aspect of becoming aware is looking out for situations where you might be confusing people or circumstances in your current life with someone or something from the past. For instance, just because a person you know right now says or does something similar to someone you knew before, doesn't necessarily mean they're acting with the same intention. Be mindful of not wrongly loading past grievances onto someone in the here and now.

Next, you need to accept that you can't change what's already happened, whatever the perceived rights and wrongs of it all, but you can change your response, namely, how you think, feel and behave both now and in the future. This is the key to releasing the shackles of old grievances that may be stopping you from moving on.

Improve your understanding

Once you become more aware of when you're feeling resentful, it's important to get clear in your mind *what you feel resentful about,* and *why*. Your resentment may be directed towards another person and the things they said or did, or you may feel resentful towards an organisation or even a place. Whatever your focus, ask yourself what happened and why, so you're clear about the cause of your resentment.

It's also helpful if you can determine *why* the person (or organisation) acted in the way they did. You may not know the answer, but sometimes it's possible to ask them, if they haven't left the area or passed away. And if they're willing to explain, an understanding of what motivated them can help ease the emotional burden you've been carrying. It doesn't make them any less responsible for something they may have said or done, but it often puts what happened into context and helps you move on.

Sometimes, it also turns out that their motivation was not what you thought it was. Yes, it may have been a deliberate attempt to hurt, but any number of other possible explanations could apply. For instance, they may have been under intense pressure and their temper just overflowed. Or they may feel bad about themselves and have the habit of hitting out at others. It's not necessarily personal, just a reflection of their inner state.

However, if you can't establish the underlying motivation of the person who hurt and angered you, it's important not to jump to conclusions, because there's a risk of making erroneous assumptions. Do your best to accept that you may never know their real motivation. And importantly, this shouldn't stop you from moving on.

Next, you need to dig deep and be honest with yourself about *how the incident affected you at the time*, noting down your thoughts and feelings as you remember them, and also the impact in terms of *any actions you decided to take (or not take).* Then, even more importantly, you need to be honest about *how your resentment continues to affect you right now*. Again, note down your thoughts; not only your internal dialogue, but also the tone of voice you use when speaking to yourself, and any distressing pictures that may flash across your conscious mind, because these things impress great depth of feeling on your subconscious. Record how this actually makes you feel, and finally, how you behave.

What you're trying to determine is the effect the incident has had on things such as how you view the world and other people, what you think you can accomplish, your happiness, peace of mind and so on. When resentment has built up, there's a risk of getting stuck in a certain way of thinking and acting, particularly when there's a repeat or similar episode to something that's happened before.

Moving on

Finally, ask yourself two questions: *what can I do differently now?* And: *how can I move on*? Both of these fire up your sub-conscious to help you find ways of letting go of any resentment you may be holding onto. You also empower yourself to start thinking and behaving differently. This may involve, for instance, speaking up where you remained silent before, or stepping bravely up to the plate rather than letting your fears hold you back.

If right now, you're feeling a bit apprehensive about making these sorts of changes, just keep in mind that actually going through this process helps transform how you think and feel about any resentment that's built up in your life, and can motivate you to behave more constructively when someone treats you in an unacceptable way. In other words, when you change your internal dialogue and the pictures you visualise in your mind, it makes you feel more upbeat. You're then able to take the sort of action that will help you put your resentment aside. Some of the affirmations mentioned in Chapter 6 may also help facilitate this transition.

FORGIVING OTHERS

Another aspect of putting blame and resentment behind us is being able to forgive those who have hurt or wronged us in some way.

But before we get down to the nitty gritty, I'd like to talk about what forgiveness is, and what it isn't.

Forgiveness is not pretending that an upsetting incident wasn't really that bad or didn't have any effect on us. It is not condoning what happened, nor is it implying that we should forget and erase it from our minds. It is not allowing an offence to occur again and again, nor is it letting the offender off the hook. And it does not infer that we have to be reconciled with the other person.

Instead, forgiveness is letting go of all the old hurts and any thoughts of getting even or exacting punishment, so that we can move on and get the most out of our lives.

The challenge

If you've been badly hurt by someone, particularly if it's someone close to you, it can be very difficult to let go of the pain and move on. But if you're not careful, you can get so wrapped up in what happened that it takes over your thoughts and stops you from enjoying the present. The more you dwell on what happened, the more you run the risk of becoming angry and bitter. And if this happens, it can affect all areas of your life.

The act of forgiveness needs to be an honest, heartfelt process; it's not about going through the motions. Genuinely forgiving another person for the distress they caused you is an act of kindness to yourself, because it helps relieve all the hurt you've been carrying around inside, and frees you up to enjoy life and find some peace of mind. It doesn't usually happen overnight, but you can gradually develop a sense of mental and emotional well-being if you gently persist.

Start by recognising that you have a choice. As hard as it may be to accept, you don't have to continue to lead a life dominated by bitterness and old resentment. And yet forgiveness is not something that you should feel under pressure to do. When pain is fresh, it's very hard to forgive. Wait until you're ready to start work on sincerely forgiving the person who has hurt you, but don't wait forever, because unresolved hurts eat away at your happiness and inner peace.

Sort out exactly what happened and why

Get clear in your mind what happened and why it was unacceptable, as well as how you feel about it and how you reacted. It's also helpful to acknowledge how the experience is adversely affecting your life right now, and what the benefits would be if you could let it go. Be as honest as you can.

It may help to talk about it with a trusted friend or family member, or to write down in a journal all your thoughts and feelings about what happened and why you're upset. Both talking and writing help to work through your thoughts and emotions associated with the experience.

Put yourself in the other person's shoes and try to understand why they did what they did. You're not trying to excuse them, but understanding the reasons for their actions can sometimes make it easier to forgive and move on. Do your best not to condemn the other person outright. Instead, try to discern the reasons for their actions. Often people are just doing the best they can, although it may not feel like it from your point of view. What happens is that their fears and insecurities cause them to behave in a way that hurts and offends those around them. Just to emphasise, you're not trying to excuse whatever they did, but if you can recognise their shortcomings and start to understand the context in which they acted, it's easier to forgive them.

Stop replaying the hurt

The next step is to stop replaying all the hurt inside your head and let go of any desire to punish the other person. Mentally replaying all the hurt over and over again stops the wound from healing and makes it more difficult to move forward in your life. If your mind keeps flitting back to how you've been wronged, gently switch your thoughts to something more positive; you achieve nothing productive by going over it all again and again.

I do appreciate that when you've been badly hurt, it's sometimes easier said than done to put it out of your mind. If that's the case, try switching your thoughts to one of these affirmations:

I am kind, gentle, loving and forgiving
I choose to heal and forgive
Forgiveness is part of my nature
I set myself free by choosing to forgive
I am free to get the best out of life

As you say a calming affirmation to yourself – or out loud – try to use a soothing tone of voice and picture a calming image in your mind's eye. If to begin with, this proves too difficult, listen to some soothing music or look at a calming photo or video.

If you find that you're overwhelmed with a desire to get even, tell the other person exactly what you think of them or punish them for what they've done, you need to do your very best to let go of those thoughts…not for their sake, but for yours. Try using the guided imagery in Chapter 6. Revenge is not satisfying and doesn't compensate for what actually happened; it only saps your energy and drags you down. While you're focusing on getting even, you can't move your own life forward in a positive way; you suffer far more than the person who hurt you.

Learning from the experience

Identify what you have learnt from the experience. In particular, think about what you could do differently if faced with a similar situation again. It's important to not only try and change your thoughts and the associated feelings, but also to change how you behave, i.e. what actions you take. What you decide to do will obviously vary from situation to situation, but remember you don't have to be dragged down and immobilised by what happened.

Put your energies into moving your life forward rather than replaying the experience that hurt you over and over again. Think about ways you can accomplish what you want and take the first step to move on from what happened. As you take that first tentative step, it's then easier to take the second step, and so on. As you build up a bit of momentum, you'll find you can let go of old grudges and make way for hope and peace of mind.

What if I can't forgive?

Finally, you may be thinking: *I can't forgive.* If you've been badly hurt by someone, it can take time to let go of what happened. Old resentments are going to creep back into your mind, and you may find yourself getting angry and upset all over again. If this happens, don't feel discouraged or give up. Remember, you are forgiving the other person, primarily for your own sake, irrespective of whether or not they ask for forgiveness, repent or change their ways. You need to free yourself from what happened so you can move on and do what you want to do in your life. When old grudges crowd your mind and you feel stuck, just be patient with yourself and revisit this step-by-step process. I know it's hard, but you can make it through.

KEY POINTS

If blame and resentment are an issue in your life, keep the following in mind:

Blame

1. On the face of it, blaming others absolves you of responsibility. If someone else is to blame, then you can say: *it's not my fault, I couldn't help it,* and so on.
2. But, regardless of who is responsible and to what extent, you are not doing yourself any favours by blaming others for what happened. The minute you do that, you take on the mantle of a victim, someone who has no choice but to accept the outcome.
3. When you feel you have no control over a situation, and are unable to influence what's happening, you get stuck and find it difficult to move on. So, in the interests of your mental and emotional well-being, it's essential to avoid the blame game.
4. What's needed is an approach that switches your focus from finding fault and conveying recriminations to identifying what can be done right now to improve things and avoid something similar happening in the future.

Resentment

5. Resentment is typically triggered by someone you know saying or doing something you consider to be hurtful, disrespectful or in some way unacceptable. It can also be sparked if you believe someone has *not done* all that you feel they *should have done*; this is obviously subjective, and varies from person to person.
6. It's part of human nature to mentally revisit upsetting experiences as a way of processing and coming to terms with what's happened, but this thought process needs to be constructive.
7. Typically, what happens when going over resentful thoughts again and again is that you believe you'll somehow gain the justice you think you're owed. What you're doing is hanging on to the need to be right, which can stop you from letting go of the hurt and anger, and finding some peace of mind.

8. Revenge is not sweet and doesn't lead to fulfilment or peace of mind. You achieve nothing by trying to get even with the other person, or proving you're right and they're wrong.

9. The way to deal with both blame and resentment is to apply the 5-step process.

Forgiving Others

10. It is important to be clear about what forgiveness is, and what it isn't. It is not pretending that an upsetting incident wasn't really that bad. It is not condoning what happened, nor is it implying that you should forget what happened. It is not allowing an offence to occur again, nor is it letting the offender off the hook. It does not infer that you have to be reconciled with the other person. Instead, forgiveness is letting go of all the old hurts and any thoughts of getting even or exacting punishment, so you can move on and get the most out of your life.

11. Genuinely forgiving another person for the distress they caused is an act of kindness to yourself, because it helps relieve all the hurt you've been carrying around inside, and frees you up to enjoy life and find some peace of mind. It doesn't happen overnight, but you can gradually develop a sense of mental and emotional well-being if you gently persist.

12. And yet forgiveness is not something that you should feel under pressure to do. When pain is fresh, it's very hard to forgive. It's important to wait until you're ready to start work on sincerely forgiving the person. But don't wait forever, because unresolved hurts eat away at your happiness and inner peace.

QUESTIONS

If you're having difficulty letting go of resentment, I recommend completing the following exercise, which is designed to pave the way for moving on and finding greater peace of mind.

The exercise consists of two parts:

- Eight questions to help clarify how resentment is affecting you now and what you can learn from it, and
- Seven sentences for you to complete to help you let go of the resentment, forgive and find some peace of mind.

What do you feel resentful about?

1. Who do you feel resentful towards? (This may be an individual or an organisation)
2. What do you feel resentful about and why?
3. What motivated the other person or organisation to behave in the way they did? (If you know.)
4. Did the event, situation or circumstances that caused you to feel resentful remind you of anything similar that happened in the past? If so, in what way?
5. How did it affect your thoughts, feelings and behaviour at the time?
6. And how is it affecting your thoughts, feelings and behaviour now?
7. What sort of physical reactions occur in your body when you're feeling resentful?
8. What can you learn from the experience that will help you move on?

When considering your thoughts, try to include not only your internal dialogue, but also the tone of voice you use and any pictures that may flash across the screen in your mind.

Moving On

1. I use the following affirmation to switch my internal dialogue from resentful to calming thoughts...
2. The tone of voice I use when I repeat my affirmation is…
3. This is a description of the creative visualisation I use to picture peace of mind …
4. My affirmation and visualisation encourage me to feel… (Record how you will feel emotionally when you've released the resentment, and do your best to feel those feelings).
5. In order to feel the way I want to feel, I make the following changes to my posture, facial expressions and level of tension in my face and body…
6. I listen to the following piece of music (or video) to reinforce my affirmation, visualisation and feelings…
7. The actions I'm motivated to take to release the resentment in my life, move on and find some peace of mind are…

You can also carry out a similar exercise if you want to put an end to blame.

CHAPTER 8: LETTING GO OF GUILT

Guilt is a negative emotion we experience when we believe we've said or done something that's hurt someone (or something) else. It can cause great anguish and unhappiness. It can morph into a sense of shame where we feel so bad about ourselves because of what we've done that it undermines our self-worth. If it's not dealt with properly, it can lead to an overwhelming sense of remorse that comes from continually thinking about something we dearly wish we hadn't said or done. It's therefore imperative to find ways of managing it effectively and releasing it from our lives.

We've all said and done things we regret, which have caused us to feel guilty. Maybe we made a mistake. Perhaps we were too busy thinking about ourselves and pursuing our own needs that we didn't appreciate the effect it would have on others. Maybe we did something out of a lack of experience. Perhaps we acted rashly in the moment and simply didn't think through the implications of what might happen. Or maybe we were tempted to deliberately hurt someone, because of something they had said or done 'to us'. Whatever the circumstances, in the interests of those we may have wronged, as well as our own self-respect and well-being, we cannot allow guilt to fester. But before focusing on how to deal with it, it's important to be clear about the nature of guilt.

TYPES OF GUILT

Guilt comes in many different forms, but the most easily recognisable is feeling guilty for something we have **actually said or done**, i.e. there was a specific action on our part that has led to a sense of guilt. This may involve other people where our words or actions resulted in them being hurt or wronged in some way. But it may also result from violating our own principles and values, such as lying or cheating. Or maybe we did something we declared we would never do again like overeating, drinking too much alcohol or leaving a pet at home all day.

The next type of guilt comes from **not doing what we feel we *ought* to be doing**. This might include not contacting family and friends as often as we feel we should, not going to the gym or not recycling. But it can also cover situations where we are caring for a sick or elderly relative, or supporting friends who are going through a difficult time. In the latter examples, we may have devoted a huge amount of time caring for or supporting those involved, but find we can't continue, because it's starting to interfere with our own life, stopping us from fulfilling our own obligations or adversely affecting our health and well-being. And yet, we still feel guilty because we believe we ought to be doing more.

Then, there is guilt that is derived from **thoughts we perceive to be improper, but which we don't act out**. We may have considered behaving in a way that is dishonest or unfaithful, or in some other way contrary to our principles and values. And although we don't literally act out those thoughts, they can still provoke a sense of guilt because they're contrary to all that we hold dear.

And finally, there are those **thoughts and actions that we believe *might* have had an adverse outcome,** and for which we feel responsible, so we're consumed with guilt. For instance, we might find ourselves wishing that a difficult colleague would experience a harmful turn of events, so that we no longer have to deal with her. Then if that should come to pass, we start to believe it was due to our own malevolent thoughts. Although part of us knows this is illogical, we might nevertheless find it hard to rid ourselves of the belief that we're somehow responsible.

Similarly, if we're responding calmly and assertively to an insult that has just been lobbed in our direction, and a well-meaning friend wades in and starts shouting at the offender, maybe even jostling or hitting the other person, we may be tempted to think we're responsible for our friend's actions, when in fact, we didn't request the intervention.

It is evident that feelings of guilt are very subjective, and may even be considered illogical, but they are very real, and can result in great torment if not managed effectively.

STRATEGIES FOR HANDLING GUILT THAT DON'T WORK

When guilt sets in, some people have a tendency to try and ignore it, or suppress it, in the hope that it will go away. The problem with this approach, however, is that it's nothing more than denial, and anything that's left unresolved has the habit of cropping up again, often at the most inopportune moments. Try as they might to stop thinking about what they have done or feel they should have done, the feelings of guilt come crashing into their everyday life, disrupting their happiness and peace of mind.

Other people might be tempted to try and cover up what's happened, particularly if they don't know how to right the wrong. Apart from the fact that there's always the risk of being 'found out' if they don't own up, this approach does nothing for their self-respect and self-worth.

At the opposite end of the spectrum, some people find that their perceived guilt may lead to a belief that they don't deserve to move on and be at peace, and that they should feel guilt-stricken forevermore, as a punishment for what they've said or done. This attitude is particularly destructive and doesn't accomplish anything other than sabotaging all hopes and dreams. It also doesn't help those close to them.

None of these tactics are particularly helpful, because they only sap the person's energy and keep them stuck in a bad place, as well as undermining their self-esteem and preventing them from finding some peace of mind.

LETTING GO OF GUILT

If you are stricken with guilt, the key to dealing with it is to acknowledge what happened, accept responsibility, take remedial action and learn from the experience. When this happens, you may still feel bad about what about you said and did (or what you did not say or do), but in time you can move on from those negative feelings, because you've been honest and taken action to redress the situation. In other words, your past mistakes don't have to hold you back in life or destroy your chances of finding some peace of mind.

Owning up

The first step in moving on from guilt is to admit your mistake or wrongdoing. If you're someone who has a lot of regrets, then just concentrate on the main ones. When you look back, you can often see patterns in what you've said and done, so it may be more helpful to think about the types of behaviour you've exhibited rather than individual regrets. It can take a lot of courage to admit you've done something wrong, but equally it takes a lot of mental and emotional energy trying to keep it under wraps.

Acknowledge without making excuses

In admitting that you've done something wrong, it's important to acknowledge what you said or did without making any excuses. Sometimes there may be a temptation to try and justify your actions, but for whatever reason, you said what you said, or did what you did.

If your words or actions affected other people, start by asking yourself if the other person is aware of what you did. If they're not aware, you need to decide whether you're going to tell them. As a general rule, I would advise coming clean, because it's much better that they hear it from you rather than someone else. Also, by taking responsibility in this way, your self-respect goes up a notch, because you've not tried to dodge the issue. Having said that, there may be situations where you judge that it's better not to tell the person concerned, perhaps because it would cause them great pain. If this is the case, however, make sure that your reason for not saying anything is out of consideration for them, and not because it's the easy option from your own point of view. Before you decide against saying anything, you need to be as certain as you can be that the issue won't surface at some point in the future.

Give a heartfelt apology

If the person is aware of what you've done, the next thing to consider is whether you're going to apologise. Again, I believe it's the best thing to do, because it can be beneficial for both of you. That being said, there are a couple of caveats I would add. First, if your apology is likely to rake up old hurts from the past and cause the other person a lot of distress, then it may be kinder not to say anything. Secondly, if you do intend to apologise, let it be a heartfelt apology and not just a case of saying: *I'm sorry,* because it's something you feel you ought to do.

So, what makes a heartfelt apology?

- Talk to the person concerned about the wrong you did to them, and explain why you think it was wrong, as well as why you did what you did. Be honest about everything that happened.
- Let the other person talk about how they think and feel about everything that took place, and really listen to what they have to say.
- Make a genuine apology, acknowledging how they think and feel about what happened, e.g. *I'm sorry I hurt you, I'm sorry what I did made you angry, I'm sorry I put you in a difficult position.* When you acknowledge their feelings and express genuine regret, it shows you've taken on board how your actions have affected them.
- Promise that whatever happened won't happen again.
- Establish if there's anything you can do to rectify or make up for your actions. If there is, then be prepared to follow through, providing it's within reason, not contrary to your values nor likely to hurt anyone else. If you're not comfortable with what you're being asked to do, then explain why and see if there's anything you can do instead.

More than anything else, your apology needs to be sincere, and you need to convey that you understand the consequences of your actions. If you just go through the motions, saying the words but not really meaning it, the recipient will see right through you.

It's also important to avoid excessive apologies, where you apologise four or five times, pointing out at the same time how bad you feel. This sort of apology is all about you and your feelings, rather than acknowledging the impact of your actions on the other person, trying to rectify the wrong and (if appropriate) repairing the rift.

Another aspect of extending an apology is that you need to consider whether it's best handled face-to-face, over the phone or in writing. This will depend on the circumstances and whether the person you've wronged is willing to meet or speak with you. There may also be situations where those involved have passed away or you no longer have contact with them. In such instances, one option is to write them a letter – although it will obviously never be sent – acknowledging your actions and the effect on them. This can be very cathartic.

Finally, be prepared for the fact that your apology may not be well received by the other person. Interestingly, those affected often do appreciate the fact that you've come clean and respect you for doing so, but there's no guarantee; it depends on the circumstances and the person concerned. The important thing from your own point of view, however, is that when you acknowledge you did something wrong and extend a sincere apology, you can look yourself in the eye, because you've not tried to duck your responsibilities. This also helps facilitate moving on from the guilt and regret.

Right the wrong

As much as you might want to change what you said or did, you can't undo what's been done, but you may be able to make amends for your actions.

Sometimes there's a straightforward way to make up for a wrongdoing, such as paying for the repair of property that's been damaged. But more often than not, you can't directly right the wrong. For instance, if you've betrayed a confidence or cheated on someone, these matters are not so easily fixed.

Think carefully about how you can make amends. If it's appropriate, you may want to ask the person you've wronged if there's anything you can do to make up for it. If the person concerned is likely to be upset by such an approach or inclined to reject it outright, you may be able to make reparations anonymously. For instance, you might consider making a donation to a charity they support, or volunteering your time in support of that good cause.

What if nobody else is involved?

If the only person who has been adversely affected by your actions is you yourself, perhaps because you acted contrary to your values and beliefs, you still need to be open and honest about what happened and why.

Acknowledge what you said or did that you believe to be wrong, as well as why you think it was wrong, why you did what you did and how it has affected you. Apologise to yourself. Make a promise that it won't happen again. Then consider if there's anything you can do to rectify or make up for what you did and be prepared to take action to make it happen.

Learn from the experience

Part of the process of coming to terms with guilt involves accepting that you can't change what happened, but you can learn from the experience and change how you view it.

It helps to try and understand why you did what you did. While it's important to accept responsibility without making any excuses, it's also important to understand the circumstances and the context in which you acted. Perhaps you were simply out of your depth and acted in the interests of self-preservation. Maybe you were so stressed out, your judgment was affected. Or perhaps you didn't have the courage to speak up when you feel you should have done. Any number of possible explanations could apply. Just remember, we've all been there; you're not alone. When you develop an understanding of the context in which you acted, you become more mindful should similar situations arise in the future, and this provides an opportunity of doing things differently next time.

Another aspect of increasing your understanding is becoming more aware of the personal values you may have violated. One reason you may feel bad and deeply regret your actions is because you've acted in a way that goes against something that's very important to you, thereby undermining your integrity. Resolve to live in line with your values going forward.

While we're discussing values, there's another aspect to explore. Are the standards by which you are judging yourself your own values or someone else's, such as those of your parents, teachers, partner, friends or colleagues? Both when we're growing up and when we step out into the wider world, we're exposed to other people's values, some of which become our own and some of which remain the expectations of others. If you've violated values that are truly your own, then you need to learn from the experience and do your best to live by them in the future. But if you're trying to live up to someone else's expectations, the people concerned may never approve and you may sacrifice your happiness trying to seek their validation.

Take control of your internal dialogue, pictures and feelings

Perhaps the most harmful aspect of guilt is that it can become all-absorbing and literally take over your thinking time. In endeavouring to learn from what happened, you're encouraging yourself to move on, but sometimes thoughts of guilt, and perhaps deep shame, take time to shake off. If you're not mindful, self-condemnation and reproach can flood into your mind. Your internal dialogue becomes very critical, you use a harsh tone of voice to yourself, and see disparaging images flash across the screen in your mind. When this happens, you're at risk of going in a downward spiral, so it's critical to take control of those thoughts and feelings.

It's important to remember that although you may have made some mistakes you deeply regret, that doesn't mean you're 'all bad'. It doesn't cancel out the many skills and good qualities you have. If you doubt what I'm saying, make a list of all your skills and qualities right now. And if you find you can't do that because your self-esteem is at a low ebb, ask someone close to you to contribute their ideas.

Some people also go through their lives believing that they should be perfect in everything they do and say, but this simply isn't possible. Getting things wrong is part of the human condition. In darker moments, you may want to try using one of the following affirmations to help dispel negative thoughts and emotions. As you say the words to yourself – or better still, as you say them out loud – do your best to visualise them in your mind's eye and feel the associated emotion, whether it be peace and serenity, or kindness and respect. To induce a sense of calm, slow your breathing down and relax your body. And to help boost your self-respect, stand up straight, raise your head and look forward.

I am becoming a better person with each passing day
I am on the path to a better future
I treat myself with kindness and respect from this day forward
Each day I feel more at peace
I feel peace and serenity flowing through me

You can also use the guided imagery we discussed in Chapter 6 to help release guilty thoughts and feelings. This is where you visualise yourself sitting peacefully by the edge of a stream and see all your regrets gently floating away like leaves on the surface of the water until they're out of sight and gone forever.

Remember, it may take a bit of time to shed any guilt and shame you may be feeling, and to come to terms with your regrets, so be patient, and show yourself a little compassion. Think of how you would react if a friend were to confide in you about having said or done the very thing you've been chastising yourself for.

THREE SPECIAL CASES

If your sense of guilt comes from **not doing what you feel you *ought* to be doing**, in particular feeling that you should be doing more to care for a sick relative or to support a friend who is going through a tough time, you need to consider very carefully what's going on inside. Providing this type of help can take an enormous toll on your health and well-being, and you may be seriously wondering if you can carry on. And yet stacked up against this are feelings of guilt that creep in if you contemplate not continuing to provide help. It's a heart-rending dilemma. But as difficult as it is, you can actually decide whether or not to continue providing support, and if so, in what way. What matters is separating your wish to help from the guilt that may follow if you decide not to help. Keep in mind that acting out of guilt will only drag you down even more and ultimately make you less effective.

If your feeling of guilt is derived from **thoughts you may have had that were contrary to your principles and values, but on which you didn't follow through**, keep two things in mind. First, there is a big difference between thinking something improper and acting it out, and it is to your credit that you did not follow through. Secondly, like everyone else, you're human and are sometimes going to have thoughts you regret, so accept this. Rather than beating yourself up every time you find your mind focusing on what you consider to be improper, try using the guided imagery or one of the calming affirmations to help dispel negative thoughts and emotions, and reduce any temptation you may have to act out the thoughts you're concerned about.

Thirdly, if your sense of guilt is emanating from **thoughts and actions that you believe *might* have had an adverse outcome,** and for which you feel responsible, you need to establish what really happened. Not what might have happened, nor what probably happened, but what **actually** happened. If you find that something you said or did specifically led to an unfortunate outcome, then you can go through the process outlined above to deal with the guilt you're experiencing. But more often than not, when you check things out in reality, you find you are not responsible, and the feeling of guilt starts to evaporate.

FORGIVING YOURSELF

In order to move on fully from guilt and shame, you need to forgive yourself for the words or deeds that caused you to feel ashamed. And this isn't always easy.

To help with this, let's be clear about exactly what self-forgiveness is…and what it isn't. Self-forgiveness is not pretending that something you did wrong wasn't really wrong. It is not condoning your actions. It is not giving yourself free reign to carry out such actions again. And it is not implying that you should just forget about what happened and carry on regardless.

Instead, self-forgiveness is a process that involves acknowledging what you did, accepting responsibility, taking remedial action where you can and learning from the experience so you can avoid making the same mistake again. Most importantly, it is also letting go of two things:

- Any tendency to continually beat yourself up, and
- Any negative thoughts and feelings that undermine your self-esteem

...so you can move on and get the most out of life, including making a contribution to the world around you in a way that only you can do.

We've already covered how to do much of this in the earlier part of this chapter. Releasing negative thoughts about yourself can, however, be one of the most difficult things to do, particularly if you have a finely tuned conscience, so I'd like to speak a bit more about this.

If you think you don't deserve to be forgiven, and should continue to be punished, think again. You are not your mistake. You may have said or done something wrong – as we all have at some time or another – but that doesn't make you 'all bad'. You are much more than that one action. You have many skills and qualities, even if right now you may be struggling to recognise and connect with them.

Show yourself a little compassion. If you find you're going over your wrongdoing again and again, remind yourself that you have bravely accepted responsibility for what you did and are making amends in the best way you can. Then, gently switch your thoughts to something more positive, which I appreciate, is often easier said than done. I've already suggested some affirmations you may want to use, but here are three more which may resonate with you:

I am worthy of forgiveness
I am kind and gentle with myself
I am calm and at peace

As you say a positive affirmation to yourself – or out loud – try to use a soothing tone of voice and picture a calming image in your mind's eye. If, to begin with, this proves too difficult, you may want to listen to some soothing music or look at a calming photo or video.

If the spiritual aspect of life is important to you, you may wish to pray for forgiveness.

You may also want to seek forgiveness from those you have offended, but please keep in mind there is no guarantee that the other person will be willing to forgive you. In any case, this is not necessary for you to be able to move on.

Just remember that if you get stuck in your remorse, you deprive the world of the unique contribution that only you can make. Both you and those around you will benefit if you can move on.

KEY POINTS

1. There are four main types of guilt. The most easily recognisable form is feeling guilty for something we have actually said or done. The next type comes from not doing what we feel we *ought* to be doing. Then there is guilt that is derived from thoughts we perceive to be improper, but which we don't act out. And finally, there are those thoughts and actions that we believe *might* have had an adverse outcome, and for which we feel responsible.
2. Don't be tempted to ignore or suppress any guilt you might be feeling, because it has the habit of cropping up again, often at the most inopportune moments, disrupting your happiness and peace of mind.
3. If you're overwhelmed with guilt, the first step in letting go is to admit your wrongdoing and acknowledge what you said or did without making any excuses. If the only person who has

been adversely affected by your actions is you yourself, perhaps because you acted contrary to your values and beliefs, you still need to be open and honest about what happened and why.

4. As a general rule, if other people are involved, it is usually better to come clean if they are not already aware of what you have done, and extend a sincere apology. As much as you might want to change what you said or did, you can't undo what's been done, but you may be able to make amends.

5. Part of the process of coming to terms with guilt involves learning from the experience, so that you can respond differently next time round.

6. Perhaps the most harmful aspect of guilt is that it can become all-absorbing and literally take over your thinking time. Therefore, it's important to take control of your internal dialogue and the pictures on the screen in your mind. One way of doing this is to use calming affirmations to help dispel negative thoughts and emotions.

7. In order to fully move on from guilt and shame, you need to forgive yourself for the words or deeds that caused you to feel ashamed.

8. Self-forgiveness is a process that involves acknowledging what you did, accepting responsibility, taking remedial action where you can and learning from the experience so you can avoid making the same mistake again. It is also letting go of any tendency to continually beat yourself up, and any negative thoughts and feelings that undermine your self-esteem, so you can move on and get the most out of life, including making a contribution to the world around you in a way that only you can.

9. It may take a bit of time to shed your guilt and shame, and to come to terms with your regrets, so be patient, and show yourself a little compassion.

QUESTIONS

If you're finding it difficult to let go of any guilt or shame that you might be feeling, I suggest completing the following exercise, which is designed to help you learn from the experience and find a way to move on from whatever you regret.

The exercise consists of two parts:

- Eight questions to help clarify how guilt is affecting you now and what you can learn from it, and
- Seven sentences for you to complete to help you come to terms with your guilt and identify how you can move on.

Dealing with Guilt and Shame

1. What do you feel guilty about, and why?
2. What were your motives for acting in the way you did?
3. How did your actions affect yourself and others?
4. How are those actions affecting your own thoughts, feelings and behaviour now? (When considering your thoughts, try to include not only your internal dialogue, but also the tone of voice you use and any pictures that may flash across the screen in your mind.)
5. What sort of physical reactions occur in your body when you think about your actions?
6. How are those actions affecting your outlook and what you believe you can do in your life right now?
7. How can you make amends?
8. What can you learn from the experience that will help you move on?

Moving On

1. I use the following affirmation to switch my internal dialogue from guilt and shame to kind, forgiving thoughts that encourage inner peace...
2. The tone of voice I use when I repeat my affirmation is…
3. This is a description of the creative visualisation I use to help restore some inner peace…
4. My affirmation and visualisation encourage me to feel… (Record how you will feel emotionally when you've let go of the guilt and shame, and do your best to feel those feelings).
5. In order to feel the way I want to feel, I make the following changes to my posture, facial expressions and level of tension in my face and body…
6. I listen to the following piece of music (or video) to reinforce my affirmation, visualisation and feelings…
7. The actions I'm motivated to take to put guilt and shame behind me so that I can find inner peace are… (If you get stuck on this one, refer back to what you have learnt and how you can make amends.)

CHAPTER 9: BUILDING SELF-CONFIDENCE

One of the main reasons we worry is that we doubt our ability to deal with the difficult situations we're facing. The aim of this chapter is to explore how to replace self-doubt with a quiet, solid inner confidence that helps deal with situations where we believe there's an inherent risk or a threat to our well-being.

THE IMPACT OF SELF-DOUBT

Inner doubt usually manifests itself as a troubling, pervasive voice in the back of our heads that casts doubt on our ability to accomplish a task, have a difficult conversation, take on a new challenge or seize an opportunity. The tell-tale signs include self-talk like: *it's really difficult, I'm not sure I can do it* and *it's far too risky*. It may also take the form of a fear about not being able to cope with something that *might* happen, e.g. *might* make a mistake, *might* make a fool of myself, *might* take the wrong job, *might* not have enough money, and so on. Often these troubling thoughts are accompanied by worst case scenario pictures on the screen in our minds.

The seeds of doubt are often sown in childhood or as a result of the various experiences we've gone through in life. If we're constantly criticised and told we're not good enough, not capable or in some other way lacking, these criticisms can be internalised, with the result that we doubt ourselves in a way that holds us back and prevents us from doing all that we're capable of.

If we feel overwhelmed by what we're facing, self-doubt can make us feel inadequate and can undermine our confidence to deal with the challenge. This, in turn, may cause us to procrastinate, avoid doing the things we need to do or make us wary of exploring new opportunities. If this happens, there's a real risk that we'll keep taking defensive action to avoid possible failure, thereby limiting our personal growth and ability to change.

The good news, however, is that if we confront our self-doubt head-on and build up a track record of overcoming it, we become much less susceptible to its influence going forward.

So, let's explore how to do that.

BUILDING SELF-CONFIDENCE

Self-confidence is the complete opposite of self-doubt. It's an inner 'knowing' that you can handle whatever life throws at you. You *know* you can overcome your fears and come out the other side. You *know* you can solve the problems you're facing. You *know* you can handle conflict, leave a relationship that's not working, start a business, speak in front of an audience, learn a new technology or do whatever you need to do to move your life forward. You're at ease with yourself, because you *know* you can deal with whatever comes your way.

Self-confidence isn't a skill that the lucky few have; it's a skill everyone can develop. It's just a case of knowing how to do it and then doing it.

If you think about it, there are probably some areas in your life right now where you feel completely confident and relaxed about doing whatever needs to be done. You're not fazed by what lies ahead of you. And yet there may be other areas where you feel apprehensive, if not downright scared about what you have to do. For instance, you might be brilliant at standing up to your difficult boss but the thought of organising a dinner party may fill you with horror. Or you might be totally relaxed about travelling to another country, but the prospect of uploading a new app onto your iPad paralyses you on the spot.

What you need to realise is that you can build confidence in every area of your life, even if it doesn't feel like it right now. And as you do, you overcome doubts and fears that may be holding you back. You can start to do more of the things that matter to you. And you can make your dreams come true rather than being held back by a fear of failure or a sense of not being up to it.

What makes this all so exciting is that each time you develop a little more courage and confidence in a particular area of your life, you face down doubts and fears that enable you to accomplish something you previously thought you couldn't do. This newfound success then encourages you to take another brave step that leads to still more success and yet more confidence.

Building inner confidence can, quite literally, transform your life. It doesn't mean you'll never have doubts and fears again, but it does mean you can develop a tolerance of uncertainty and – most importantly – a trust in yourself that you can handle whatever comes along. Then each time you do this and successfully come out the other side, your confidence and self-esteem go up a notch. You get a warm glow of satisfaction inside that comes from facing up to and overcoming something you found difficult.

STEP 1: ACKNOWLEDGE YOUR SELF-DOUBT AND GET TO KNOW YOURSELF BETTER

You can't overcome something until you acknowledge its presence in your life, so you need to be totally honest with yourself and resist the temptation to deny any doubts you may be feeling.

You may already be aware of an aspect in your life where you lack confidence, which is great, because once it's out in the open, you can deal with it. But keep in mind that self-doubt sometimes operates in a very stealthy way under the guise of what seems like a perfectly acceptable reason for not taking a particular course of action. Our minds are very adept at coming up with excuses about why we can't do something that we know, deep in our hearts, we should be doing. For example, we don't have enough time, or we feel too tired. So be on the lookout for any doubts that might be lurking under the surface.

Often when you're racked with doubt, there can be a tendency to overlook your many skills and qualities, as well as all the things you've already accomplished.

Take some time to write down all the things you're good at, because your strengths are almost certainly in the areas of your life where you already have a lot of self-confidence. Maybe you're a great scratch cook, you're good with numbers, you're a brilliant project manager or you get on well with children. Take some time to think about all aspects of your life and make a note of what you do well.

Then think about all the things you've accomplished, whether it's passing an exam, learning to drive, travelling overseas, getting a promotion or raising three children. Again, write down everything you can think of.

As you reflect on the list of what you're good at, and all the things you've accomplished, you'll feel your confidence and self-esteem start to go up.

Finally, think about those areas of your life where you're not particularly strong but which you need to master because they're part of your everyday family, social or working life. Maybe you need to learn how to cook nutritional meals, speak up confidently in large gatherings or develop technical skills if your job involves using new apps. Whatever it is, write it down.

And, remember, no-one is perfect, even the most accomplished people you can think of. As you start to record the things you feel you're not very good at, keep everything in perspective. You are not your perceived shortcomings; they don't define you; they only undermine your confidence if you let them.

If you don't know how to make your own clothes, it's not a shortcoming if you buy them instead. If you have an artistic leaning and no understanding of computers, it's not a shortcoming if you call in an IT expert when your computer crashes. Recognise that your skills and qualities lie in a different direction. On the other hand, if your job requires you to attend meetings and you don't like walking into a room of full of people because you suddenly become tongue tied, this is something you can work on and overcome.

If you think about an aspect of your life where you're already confident, there was probably a time when you didn't have much confidence in that area at all; you had to nurture and develop it. For example, you might be a brilliant scratch cook and can rustle up a tasty meal from whatever's left in the fridge. But there may have been a time when the thought of preparing a meal without a recipe book would have filled you with apprehension. Similarly, there's no reason why you can't develop confidence in those areas of your life where you don't feel particularly strong right now.

As you go through this process, resist any temptation to compare yourself to other people. If you do this, there can be a tendency to compare the worst things you know about yourself with the best things you see in others. This isn't a fair comparison at all and only leads to despondency and feelings of inadequacy. So please, don't do it!

STEP 2: TAKE CONTROL OF YOUR INTERNAL DIALOGUE AND THE TONE OF VOICE YOU USE

At this stage in the book, it won't come as a surprise to hear that a key step in building self-confidence is to replace negative thoughts about your perceived shortcomings with hopeful thoughts about what you *can be* and *do*.

Doubts and fears make themselves known in a variety of ways, but typically, you can spot them if you find your internal dialogue includes comments like: *I can't do it, I don't know how, I won't ever be able to, I'm scared* and *what if?* At the same time, you may also find that the tone of voice you use is anxious or helpless, while awful pictures flash across the screen in your mind's eye. None of this is good news for your well-being. It only makes your doubts and fears take a firmer hold in your conscious and subconscious mind, as well as making it more difficult to move forward in your life.

The moment you become aware of any negative thoughts about the future, you need to switch your thoughts to the polar opposite. This isn't always easy, so try saying: *Stop!* or *Enough!* when this happens. Then consciously switch your thoughts to your ideal outcome.

One of the best ways of doing this is to replace the scary thoughts with a motivational affirmation. My absolute favourite is *I can do it!* It's so simple and yet so powerful. And as you say it to yourself – or, better still, as you say it out loud – put some real oomph into the words. Say it as though you really believe it!

Alternatively, you may want to replace your doubts with something like:

I am a confident person; every day my confidence increases to new heights
My intuition guides me every step of the way
I am grateful I can learn all I need to know
I am outgoing and confident in social situations.
I always express my thoughts and ideas with confidence
I can do anything I set my mind to
I have great strength of character and achieve all I set out to do

As you repeat your chosen affirmation to yourself, say it with an upbeat, motivational tone of voice, as though you really mean it and believe what you're saying.

STEP 3: CREATE CONFIDENT PICTURES ON THE SCREEN IN YOUR MIND

At the same time, visualise yourself successfully accomplishing whatever it is you've set out to do. See yourself walking confidently into a crowded room, or facing up to your inconsiderate partner or speaking up in a meeting. Paint a picture of the new confident you in your mind's eye.

If at first, your affirmation doesn't feel right, or you find yourself saying: *it's just not true*, this is simply because your old thinking habits are trying to resist the change. Gently persist, because you will gradually start to believe you can do what you previously thought you couldn't. The more you say your affirmations and visualise successfully carrying them out, the more you'll start to feel upbeat and able to overcome the apprehension of what lies ahead. If you find this difficult, listen to some inspirational music or watch an uplifting video to help motivate you to move forward in your life.

What you're aiming to do by changing your thoughts is break down your old thinking habits and change your belief system. You're endeavouring to stop discouraging thoughts from bubbling up and breaking into a stream of inner doubts that keep flooding through your mind. Be mindful about what's going on inside your head. The minute you notice that nagging, doubtful voice trying to take over, subdue it by focusing on your new affirmation, while at the same time, creating positive pictures in your mind's eye. The more you can do this, the more hopeful and motivated you'll feel about dealing with whatever challenges you're facing in life.

Another technique you might find helpful is to change the voice of your internal critic to that of Donald Duck. This may sound a bit off the wall, but what you're trying to do is subdue your doubts and fears. Would you take criticism from Donald Duck seriously!? Probably not. Doing this may even make you laugh, which also helps ease the tension. So, give it a try.

STEP 4: FEEL THE CONFIDENCE

When you think passionately about something, you give enormous power to the thought, which in turn affects how you feel. But if you've been full of self-doubt, the chances are you may be finding it difficult to 'feel' the confidence that your affirmations and the pictures on the screen in your mind are endeavouring to build. You can help things along by changing your body language.

If you're feeling apprehensive, you may well be 'shrinking' your stature as you sit or stand. You may be leaning forward, curving your spine, looking down and possibly folding your arms. To help create real confidence, stand up straight, pull your shoulders back, raise your head and look straight ahead. This simple change in posture helps induce a feeling of confidence that synchronises with your affirmations and the associated pictures inside your head. Your thoughts and feelings then feed off each other in a positive way, so that you really do start to feel more confident.

The more assured and upbeat you feel, the more you're encouraged to step up to the plate and deal confidently with situations that you previously might have shied away from.

STEP 5: GET READY, THEN BE BRAVE AND TAKE THE PLUNGE

In order to overcome and master the thing you're concerned about, you also need to prepare thoroughly. This can be anything from thinking through what you want to say to your partner to studying for new skills. In fact, it applies to every aspect of life. The more you prepare and practice, the more confidence you will have in yourself to successfully accomplish whatever you need to do or say. Whatever you're planning, prepare in advance and build the level of competence you need to succeed.

One of the best ways of doing this is to find a role model and learn from them. If possible, talk to them. Alternatively, read or listen to any material or programs they may have published about what you want to accomplish. Find out not only the actions they take and how they behave, but also what they value and believe. Getting to know their attitudes and beliefs, and *how* they do things, is as important as discovering *what* they actually do and say in certain circumstances.

One very important point here: make sure the role model you choose is an expert in their field. Don't be tempted to make do by having a quick chat with your best friend's brother, simply because he seems to know a bit about the topic you're trying to master. If your best friend's brother really is an expert in what you want to learn, then great, but if not, find someone who is. Learn only from the best.

Another effective way of building your competence is to use role play to prepare and practice. This is an appropriate technique for any situation requiring interaction with one or more people. It simply involves a run-through of the speech you're planning to give or the difficult conversation you need to have with a member of your family or one of your colleagues. It often allows you to anticipate and plan your response to difficult questions. You may want to do the role play in the privacy of your own room, or with a trusted friend or relative who can encourage, support and make helpful suggestions.

There may be instances where you can quickly build the competence you need, such as learning how to best approach your boss about a tricky matter you want to discuss. On other occasions, you may need to devote weeks or months of your time to learning a new skill. If this is the case, just take one step at a time, gradually building both your competence and confidence. As you do this, remember to use positive self-talk and visualisation, as well as adopting a confident posture, to reinforce the process and help create a successful outcome.

The final step in building self-confidence is to take action and put into practice what you've been mentally planning and preparing for.

What you're likely to discover is that all your preparation creates momentum that drives you forward; it motivates you to step bravely outside your comfort zone, even if it's something you've not done before. Yes, you might feel a little bit of trepidation, but that's not a bad thing, because it keeps you alert and on your toes. You may even find you feel a frisson of excitement.

If the fear of failure or making a fool of yourself causes you to hesitate at this point, just remember you've done lots of preparation; you're well equipped to carry out the task in front of you. Just say to yourself: *I can do it,* and take the plunge.

Stepping outside your comfort zone is one of the best ways of overcoming self-doubt. The more you do it, the more your self-confidence grows. The more real-life experience you gain, the more you accomplish, whether it's managing a difficult situation or achieving the dream of a lifetime. And the more you accomplish things you previously thought were impossible, the more it encourages you to step out bravely next time around. You keep on learning and growing.

Don't be tempted to stay permanently within your comfort zone, afraid of what might happen if you step outside. When you're faced with something daunting, it might feel like the safest option, but it isn't, because your doubts and fears only grow inside your mind. The minute you decide to face up to those fears, unseen forces have a habit of coming to your aid and you find the courage you need to do what you've been dreading. And each time you confront your doubts and fears, your confidence goes up a notch.

So, prepare and take action…again and again. It's one of the best ways of overcoming self-doubt, building confidence and accomplishing more of what you want in life.

DON'T BE DISAPPOINTED IF IT DOESN'T GO AS WELL AS YOU WOULD LIKE

There are going to be times when you step out bravely and things don't go as well as you would have liked. If this happens, it's important not to beat yourself up or vow never to put yourself in a vulnerable situation again.

Look at it like this: you wouldn't expect to pick up a musical instrument and play it perfectly the first time around if you've not had much training or practice. And you wouldn't expect to pick up a paint brush and produce a masterpiece if you've only just learnt how to paint. It's the same with anything you tackle in life. It takes a bit of time and practice to be able to do something competently. Even then, there are going to be times when you make a mistake, simply because you're human; that happens to us all every so often.

You can give up and declare you will never put yourself in the same situation again, or you can learn from it and aim to do better next time round. The problem with giving up is that it gnaws away in the back of your mind, and does nothing for your self-confidence or self-esteem. What's more, even if you do vow never to put yourself in a similar situation again, you can't guarantee, that with life's twists and turns, it won't actually happen.

Remember, you don't have to be perfect at doing whatever lies in front of you. And if you make a mistake and something goes wrong, that doesn't make you a failure. As Zig Ziglar used to say: *failure is an event, not a person*; it's an opportunity to learn and can be life changing.

So, don't give up. Be prepared for the fact that things aren't always going to go as you might have hoped. That's life. Be willing to learn from the experience and try again. Simply ask yourself: *what can*

I do right now to improve the situation I'm facing? Or: *what can I do differently next time round?* Each time you step out bravely, you grow as a person and increase your chances of success.

FEAR OF PUBLIC SPEAKING

Throughout my career I've needed to do a lot of public speaking, which I hated when I first started out. I was literally filled with fear. *What if I fall over walking onto the podium? What if I can't remember what I was going to say? What if my voice dries up? What if I make a fool of myself? What if I don't know the answer to a question?* And on and on. I experienced every imaginable fear, which was compounded by the fact that I hated being the centre of attention.

But I loved my work. I was a researcher engaged in finding out what people thought about various social issues or commercial services, what was important to them and how things might be improved. I just loved immersing myself in the analyses and coming up with possible solutions. I couldn't have been happier, but at the end of every project, I had to present the results to the client. So, if I wanted to continue in this line of work – which I did – I had to get to grips with public speaking.

I started saying to myself: *I can do it, I can do it.* I started visualising myself speaking confidently to the audience. I asked: *how can I improve my public speaking*? I did some presentational skills training, and then practised and practised. Then, when I needed to, I stepped onto the podium and spoke. At first, it was nothing short of nerve racking, but little by little, it got easier until I could take it in my stride…and even enjoy the experience!

Best of all, every time I stepped out in front of the audience, my confidence went up a notch. I would never have forgiven myself if I'd walked away from something I loved doing simply because I hated the thought of speaking in front of a group of people.

By stepping out bravely, you discover that your worst fears seldom materialise, and even if they do, more often than not, you find you can deal with them. As a result, your self-confidence goes up even more as you realise you can handle problems that would previously have immobilised you.

Building self-confidence is an ongoing process. Just keep doing everything we've spoken about here to the best of your ability and your inner confidence will grow and be there when you need it. I know it can be difficult at first, but you'll make it through. Just be patient with yourself and take it one step at a time.

In the words of Susan Jeffers: *feel the fear and do it anyway*.

KEY POINTS

1. The seeds of self-doubt are often sown in childhood or as a result of the various experiences we've all gone through in life. If you've been constantly criticised and told you're not good enough, these criticisms are likely to have been internalised, causing you to doubt yourself in a way that holds you back and prevents you from doing all you're capable of.
2. In contrast, self-confidence is an inner 'knowing' that you can handle whatever life throws at you. You're at ease with yourself, because you *know* you can overcome your fears and come out the other side, and you *know* you can solve the problems you're facing.
3. The good news is that self-confidence isn't a skill that the lucky few have; it's a skill we all can develop.
4. The starting point is to become more aware of any self-doubts you may have. Keep in mind that self-doubt sometimes operates in a very stealthy way under the guise of what seems like a perfectly acceptable reason for not taking a particular course of action.

5. If you think about an aspect of your life where you're already confident, there was probably a time when you didn't have much confidence at all; you had to nurture and develop it. Similarly, there's no reason why you can't develop confidence in those areas of your life where you don't feel particularly strong right now.
6. A key step is to replace negative thoughts about your perceived shortcomings with hopeful thoughts about what you *can be* and *do*. Through the use of affirmations and creative visualisation, you start to break down old thinking habits and change your belief system.
7. To help create real confidence inside, adopt a confident body posture by standing up straight, pulling your shoulders back, raising your head and looking straight ahead.
8. In order to overcome and master the things you're concerned about, you need to prepare thoroughly. The more you prepare and practice, the more confidence you will have to successfully accomplish whatever you need to do. To help with this process, consider finding a role model from whom you can learn, and also use role play to build your competence.
9. The final step in building self-confidence is to take action and put into practice in real life what you've been mentally planning and preparing for.
10. Stepping outside your comfort zone is one of the best ways of overcoming self-doubt. The more you do it, the more your self-confidence grows, because you begin to realise you really can handle things that would previously have immobilised you.

QUESTIONS

If you're lacking confidence in a particular area of your life, I recommend completing the following exercise, which is designed to help overcome self-doubt, build your inner confidence and accomplish whatever it is you are concerned about.

The exercise consists of two parts:

- Seven questions to help clarify how your self-doubt is affecting you now, and
- Seven sentences for you to complete to help build your inner confidence.

Overcoming Self-Doubt

1. In what area of your life are you lacking confidence?
2. Why don't you feel confident?
3. Is this the first time you've experienced a lack of confidence in this area of your life, or is it an ongoing issue?
4. If it's an ongoing issue, how has it affected your thoughts, feelings and behaviour before?
5. How is it affecting your thoughts, feelings and behaviour now?
6. What sort of physical reactions occur in your body when you're lacking confidence?
7. And how is your lack of confidence affecting your outlook and what you believe you can accomplish?

When considering your thoughts, try to include not only your internal dialogue, but also the tone of voice you use and any pictures that may flash across the screen in your mind.

Building Inner Confidence

1. I use the following affirmation to switch my internal dialogue from self-doubt to self-confidence...
2. The tone of voice I use when I repeat my affirmation is…
3. This is a description of the creative visualisation I use to picture my growing confidence…
4. My affirmation and visualisation encourage me to feel… (Record how you will feel emotionally when you've overcome your self-doubt, and then do your best to feel those feelings.)
5. In order to develop a feeling of confidence, I make the following changes to my posture…
6. I listen to the following piece of music (or video) to reinforce my affirmation, visualisation and feelings…
7. The actions I'm motivated to take to build my confidence are … (If you get stuck on this one, ask yourself: *how can I improve my skills?* Or: *what can I do differently?*)

CHAPTER 10: MOST COMMON MISTAKES AND NEXT STEPS

Welcome to the final chapter!

We've covered a lot of ground in this book, so I would like to summarise the key learnings and run through some of the most common mistakes people make, before suggesting the next steps for you.

KEY LEARNINGS

The challenge we all face in our everyday lives is how to stop our troubles and worries from undermining our happiness and peace of mind.

We've explored all sorts of different scenarios. Perhaps your concerns stem from what happened in the past; maybe you feel resentful because of how you were treated or guilty because of something you did which you now regret. Maybe you feel overwhelmed with what's happening right now and are just not sure how to deal with it. Perhaps you are experiencing relationship difficulties, have money worries or are concerned about your health. Or maybe you're worried about the future and what it might bring.

Factors influencing worry

For each and every one of us, the difficulties we face in life – whatever they are – are very real, but remember there are four things that influence the extent to which we worry: our genetic make-up, our upbringing, the experiences we've gone through and lastly, our ability to learn new ways of dealing with worrying situations. This last point is very important, because it means that, irrespective of your personality, upbringing and past experiences, you really can learn how to deal with worry more effectively.

Change your response

Although it may not seem like it, when you're angst-ridden, the harmful effects actually come from your response to the stressful situation you're facing, not the stressful situation itself. This is sometimes very difficult to accept when you're dealing with mind-bending worries. But, by changing how you respond to your problems, and in particular, by focusing on the things you have control over, as well as different choices you can make, you can transform your worry into something more manageable. You can't change other people – only they can do that – and you often can't change the situation in which you find yourself, but you can change how you respond to others and how you deal with the situation you're facing.

Focus on the things you can control

When you're worried out of your mind, it's very easy to get locked into the belief that you've got no choice and have to accept whatever's happening to you, but that's not the case, it's only how it seems. You don't have to be dragged down by all the problems in your life.

The key to managing worry is to change the things over which you have complete control, namely:

- The way you think about your problems, which includes your internal dialogue, the tone of voice you use and the pictures you create in your mind.

- The emotional feelings your problems generate inside you.
- The behaviour you demonstrate and the actions you subsequently take.

This is the crux of it all.

Set up a force field of energy

When you take back control of your thoughts, feelings and actions, you release the shackles that have been holding you back. You discover alternative ways of dealing with stress and worry that can bring great relief, and most importantly of all, you find greater happiness and peace of mind.

The minute you start to switch your thoughts away from what you don't want (your doubts and concerns) towards what you do want (your ideal outcome), you set up a force field of energy that helps overcome your worries and accomplish what you want. This isn't make-believe, it's a reflection of the natural laws of the universe.

Mobilise the power of your subconscious

As you start to focus your conscious mind on what you want rather than on your doubts and worries, these constructive thoughts get impressed on your subconscious. And as you start to think more constructively, new ideas pop into your mind about how to resolve your difficulties…ideas that would previously have been filtered out by your deep-seated attitudes and beliefs. You become aware of all sorts of opportunities and choices that you didn't notice before. And most importantly, you start to realise you have skills and qualities you thought you didn't have.

Together, these things create a new understanding of yourself and the world around you, causing you to feel more upbeat, so you're motivated to take action to sort out the problems you're facing. And when this happens, you start to see real, positive change manifest itself in your external life, leading to more favourable outcomes.

Your subconscious is the powerhouse that operates beyond your conscious awareness. It's a truly phenomenal part of your being, and has an amazing capacity to come up with ideas and solutions to the difficulties in your life, but its efforts have to be channelled in the right direction. And the way to do this is via your conscious mind, because your subconscious simply accepts any information it's given by your conscious mind.

What this means from the point of view of resolving your troubles and worries is that if you can replace the worry-type thoughts in your conscious mind with more upbeat thoughts, you can reprogram your subconscious to do two things. First, to attract all sorts of ideas, solutions and people into your life to help overcome your concerns. And secondly, going forward, to develop more constructive attitudes and beliefs that will serve you more effectively.

Synchronise your mind and body

Another point to remember is that the brain and the body interact very closely with each other via powerful electrochemical signals. This means you can induce more positive emotions, such as a sense of calm, confidence or happiness, by changing your posture, the level of tension in your muscles and your facial expressions. By holding and moving your body in a way that mirrors the thoughts in your conscious mind, your mind and body become synchronised so you start to feel the way you think, and think the way you feel.

Implement the 5-step process

The **first step** in smoothing away your worries is to become more aware of when you're focusing on what you don't want, i.e. your concerns, doubts and fears, and how these things manifest themselves in your mind and body. There are several things to look out for. The first is your internal dialogue, which may include lots of negative thoughts, while the tone of voice you're using may be anxious or agitated. Next are the bad news pictures that may flash across the screen in your mind, reinforcing all sorts of unhelpful self-talk. And then there are physical reactions such as tightness or tension in various parts of your body, which tend to emulate a worried, dejected emotional state. And finally, worry may cause you to delay or avoid taking action that might be helpful in resolving the difficulties in your life. These all provide clues that help identify when you're in a worried state of mind.

Once you become aware of when you're thinking about what you don't want, you need to switch your focus to the polar opposite of your worries. So, the **second step** involves switching your internal dialogue and the tone of voice you're using to what you want, i.e. your ideal outcome. It's not always easy to make this switch nor sustain it, so there are two simple techniques to help with this process. The first is to ask: *how can I <solve this problem>?* to fire up your subconscious to come up with an answer to your problems. And the second is to use an affirmation to keep your mind on your ideal outcome and off the things you're worried about.

The **third step** is to use creative visualisation to replace the bad news pictures flashing across the screen in your mind with more favourable images that reflect your ideal outcome. This reinforces the changes in your internal dialogue and helps to harness the power of your imagination to bring about favourable changes in your life. If, at first, no matter how hard you try, you can't create a picture or movie of what you want inside your head, find a picture in a magazine or online that encapsulates what you ideally want and focus on that instead.

In order to smooth away your worries, your mind and body need to be synchronised. What this means is that as you switch your internal dialogue and the pictures on the screen in your mind to something more upbeat, you also need to change how you're feeling inside to something more upbeat. The **fourth step** therefore involves *feeling how you would feel* if your new thoughts – what you really want – were a reality in your life right now. One of the most effective ways of doing this is to change your posture and facial expressions to emulate the emotion you wish to feel, such as being happy and confident.

The **fifth and final step** in easing the worries out of your life is to take action to resolve the problems you're facing, which becomes much easier once you've undertaken steps 1-4. By thinking and feeling differently, you become aware of options you didn't notice before, and you see yourself in a different light. As a result, your worries no longer hold you back. You're motivated to behave differently, and this leads to more positive outcomes in your life.

Be kind to yourself

I realise it's not easy to keep your thoughts and feelings focused on what you want, so if you find your mind keeps flipping back to all your concerns, gently switch those thoughts to your chosen affirmation and the supporting pictures on the screen in your mind. Don't be tempted to beat yourself up if your mind keeps jumping back to your worries. It takes a bit of practice to kick the worry habit, so each time you notice you're dwelling on your worries, just calmly shift your thoughts to the polar opposite. At the same time, remember to adopt a posture that reflects how you want to feel, whether calm and confident, or happy and motivated. The more you can do this, the more you'll weaken the hold that worry has on your life, while at the same time, starting to embed in your subconscious a more constructive way of dealing with the problems you're facing.

As time goes on, you'll become more confident, you'll start to trust that your subconscious will find a solution to the difficulties in your life, you'll feel more upbeat, you'll be motivated to take constructive action, you'll get better outcomes and, most importantly of all, you'll find some peace of mind and develop an inner calm.

What I'd like to do now is talk about the most common mistakes people make when trying to get rid of the worry in their lives.

MOST COMMON MISTAKES

An inside job

When faced with all sorts of troubles and worries, people sometimes think that the way to get rid of their concerns is to change the situation they're in. This may involve changing their job, changing where they live, changing their partner, changing the way they spend their leisure time, and so on. And yes, there may indeed be times when making such a change is the best thing to do, but this isn't necessarily the case.

If this applies to you, first and foremost, what needs to change is what is going on inside your head by focusing on what you want.

It took me a long while to realise this in my early career. I hated all the office politics and wheeling and dealing that seemed to be going on around me, so I changed jobs every two or three years. And to my surprise, I found myself in the same sort of situation again! What I didn't realise at the time was that while I kept focusing on what I *didn't want* (all the wheeling and dealing) that was what I kept on getting.

When I spent some time thinking about what I actually *wanted* (to work in a team of like-minded, motivated people) everything changed. It changed how I felt, it changed the opportunities that apparently just came my way, it changed the choices I made, and it changed the actions I took, which in turn led to a much happier life, both in and out of work.

The point I'm emphasising here is that getting rid of worry is an inside job; the important thing is what goes on inside your head. To change what you're worried about *out there*, you have to change what's going on *in here*, which is what the 5-step process is designed to accomplish.

You think you can't change

Another common mistake that people make is thinking they can't change. They say: *I've always been a worrier and always will be.* But here's the thing: just because they've worried about everything in the past doesn't mean to say they can't change in the future.

To recap: there are four things that influence the extent to which we all worry, namely our genetic make-up, our upbringing, the experiences we've gone through, and – most importantly of all – our ability to learn new ways of dealing with worrying situations. This last point is good news for all worriers, because irrespective of what's gone before, it really is possible to get your worries under control and manage them more effectively. This has been my experience and that of countless other people as well.

I was a born worrier; in fact, I was outstanding at it. What made me change was when it started to affect my physical and emotional health. I just knew I had to find a more effective way of dealing with the stress in my life. There then followed years of research, study and real-life application, during which I learnt how to manage the worries in my life more effectively.

Problems and difficulties still come my way – that's part of life – but they don't immobilise me anymore or destroy my innate happiness and peace of mind. I know there's an answer out there; all I have to do is find it by focusing on what I want and trusting that a way forward will become clear. And it always does.

So, in response to the question, *can you really change*? The answer is definitely *yes*.

It's not working

Sometimes when people start using the sorts of techniques included in the 5-step process, they say they're not working. Let's talk a bit about this.

You may remember that all sorts of deep-seated attitudes and beliefs which have built up over our lifetime, are stored in our subconscious mind, affecting how we think and feel, as well as the actions we take and the outcomes we experience. Much of the time, these attitudes and beliefs operate below the radar, so we're completely unaware of them and how they're affecting our lives. They create a way of thinking that has become an old habit, just happening automatically.

This is fine if the attitudes and beliefs are positive, working in our best interests, but if they're negative, they can lead to all sorts of powerful doubts and worries that undermine our confidence and what we believe we can do in our lives. The good news, as already discussed, is that we can reprogram our subconscious by feeding it constructive dialogue and pictures via our conscious mind.

But the thing to recognise is that it takes time to impress a new, more constructive way of thinking onto our subconscious. None of us are going to overturn an unhelpful thinking habit that has built up over the years by saying a few affirmations and doing some visualisation for a few days. It takes longer than that. This is why it may seem as though some of the techniques in the 5-step process aren't working. They will work; it just takes a bit of time and practice.

Do your best to notice when you're dwelling on your worries, and when you realise that you are, switch your thoughts to the polar opposite. The more you can do this, the more speedily you'll start to notice when you're focusing on what you don't want.

And remember that your thoughts and feelings need to be synchronised and working in the same direction. It's not enough to switch your thoughts to what you want, you also need to feel how you would feel if your ideal outcome was already a reality. Sometimes changing your thoughts to something more upbeat will bring about a change in how you feel, but if not, change your posture and other aspects of how you hold and move your body to induce the sort of feeling you want.

Don't beat yourself up

Another common mistake people make is to beat themselves up if they find their thoughts have wandered back to all their worries rather than focusing on their desired outcome. This is closely linked to the previous issue in that it takes time to replace an old, unhelpful thinking habit with a new, more constructive one.

If your mind flips back to the very thing you're trying not to think about (your worries), just gently refocus your thoughts on what you want (your ideal outcome). Resist any temptation to beat yourself up, because this won't accomplish anything helpful at all.

You need to take action

The thoughts in our conscious mind are all powerful. If they're positive, they can transform our lives and help us deal effectively with the problems we're facing, but if they're negative, they reinforce our doubts and concerns.

But, there's more to it than that.

What happens is that our conscious mind impresses our thoughts on our subconscious, and this causes us to feel the way we feel. If we communicate constructive thoughts and pictures to our sub-conscious, we're going to feel upbeat and raring to go, but if we communicate negative thoughts and pictures, we're going to feel down and demotivated.

And then, there's yet another critical step.

Our thoughts and feelings affect our behaviour. If we're feeling upbeat, we're motivated to take action to deal with our troubles and worries. But if we're feeling down, we struggle to take any action at all. And taking fresh action is what makes all the difference, because our actions manifest themselves in the outcomes in our lives.

Thinking constructive thoughts by focusing on what we want rather than on our worries is the crucial starting point in bringing about change in our lives. But it's not enough to ask the *how can I...?* question, say a few affirmations, visualise, and then just sit back and wait. We have to take action to change things. This is a vital point that is sometimes overlooked by personal growth enthusiasts.

So, let's move on to the first thing I recommend you do right now.

SUGGESTED NEXT STEPS

Option 1

If you've been completing the exercises at the end of each chapter, that's great. The important thing now is to actually put the answers you gave into practice in real life. Keep your mind focused on what you want rather than on your doubts and concerns. If you notice your thoughts flipping back to your worries over the course of the day, just gently switch your focus to what you desire in life by asking the *how can I...?* question, or repeating your chosen affirmations and using creative visualisation. Remember as well to change your posture to reflect how you want to feel.

If this is proving to be a real challenge, try listening to some calming music or watch an uplifting video to help get your thoughts into a more positive place. And if you're finding it difficult to let go of something, try the guided imagery technique detailed in Chapter 6, where you see yourself sitting by a stream, watching your troubles float away like the leaves on the surface of the water.

Then, it's important to take fresh action to resolve the problems in your life.

Option 2

If you've not yet had a chance to complete the exercises at the end of each chapter and put the 5-step process into practice, I encourage you to make the time to do it right now. Start by completing the exercises at the end of Chapters 3, 4 and 5 and then implementing in real life the answers you've given.

- The exercise at the end of Chapter 3 helps you become more aware of any deep-seated attitudes and beliefs that may be generating all sorts of doubts and worries in your mind, and holding you back.
- The exercise at the end of Chapter 4 helps you identify and become more aware of how worry actually affects your thoughts, feelings and behaviour, and also provides a benchmark against which you can evaluate your progress going forward.
- And then, the exercise at the end of Chapter 5 shows how to

implement the 5-step process to smooth away your worries in your life. This involves switching your thoughts from what you don't want (i.e. your doubts and fears) to what you do want (i.e. your ideal outcome) by devising an appropriate affirmation and using creative visualisation to inoculate your worry, and then taking fresh action to resolve your problems. If you need to jog your memory on how to create the perfect affirmation or vivid imagery, please re-read Chapter 5.

The benefit comes from actually *doing* what we've been discussing. And if you get started right away, you can take advantage of the momentum that's been created by reading this book. If you don't start now, there's a real risk you never will.

Summing up

The key point of the 5-step process is that when you concentrate fervently on something, you give enormous power to the associated self-talk and pictures in your mind's eye. This, in turn, encourages your subconscious to go off and find answers to the problems in your life, as well as creating positive emotions associated with the ideal outcome you want to accomplish. You then start to feel more upbeat, your worries begin to diminish, and you're motivated to take action to sort out the difficulties you're facing. When this happens, you start to see real, positive change manifest itself in your external life, leading to more favourable outcomes.

I can't emphasise enough the importance of actually putting into practice the 5-step process, which is what the exercises at the end of every chapter are designed to help you do. It's important to understand the theory, but that alone will not bring about transformation; you must implement the theory in real life. You can always go back and re-read one or more of the chapters for clarification. In fact, I recommend doing that in any case, because you will almost certainly notice points you may have missed the first time around.

I know some of this stuff can be difficult, but you've got what it takes to make it through. You really can replace mind-numbing worries with tranquillity and peace of mind. It may take a bit of time to perfect the techniques, so be patient with yourself. Just keep in mind that *you can do it*, you really can.

I wish you well.

Kay Johnson

APPENDIX: EXAMPLES OF AFFIRMATIONS

When creating an affirmation, it must be personal (i.e. it includes the words 'I' or 'my'), focused on your ideal outcome and in the present tense.

If you're finding it difficult to come up with the 'right' affirmation for you, some examples are shown below. You may find the perfect affirmation here, or more likely, you'll want to tailor one or more of them, or create something totally different. What's important is that the words you choose must really resonate with you.

HEALTH

Worries

I feel exhausted all the time
I'm always going down with one cold after another
I'm worried about my health
What if I've got a life-threatening illness?
I feel so down/dejected/miserable

Suggested affirmations

I abound with good health and awake with new energy every day; I am a very healthy person
I'm brimming over with good health, energy and enthusiasm
My body heals easily and quickly
I allow life and vitality to flow through me
I am healthy, happy and radiant
I live a happy, healthy, harmonious life
My days are full of hope, health and happiness
Every day and in every way, I'm feeling better and better
I am happy, have peace of mind and am grateful for everything I have
I am calm and at peace

PROSPERITY

Most of us experience money worries at some time in our life. These affirmations are designed to help you switch from what is often described as 'scarcity thinking' to 'abundance thinking'.

Worries

I never have enough money
Money goes out faster than it comes in
I'm in debt up to my ears
What if I'm laid off?
I'm underpaid
I'm worried about my long-term financial security
It's wrong to have too much money
I don't deserve more money

Suggested affirmations

I have all the money I need to lead the life I choose
I thrive and prosper wherever I am
My income is constantly increasing
My job is safe and secure
I make a valuable contribution at my place of work
I love the work I do and am well paid for it
I have lots of choices; opportunity is everywhere
I'm worthy of a wealthy life
I allow money to flow into my life
I'm open and receptive to all the wealth life offers me

RELATIONSHIPS

Worries

I feel so lonely

I don't have many friends

Nobody loves me

I'll never find the right man/woman for me

I always mess up my relationships

What if he/she walks out on me?

Suggested affirmations

I attract loving, caring people into my life

I have a wonderful circle of caring friends

I am lovable and deeply loved

I find love/friendship wherever I turn

I give and receive love/friendship freely and happily

My ideal man/woman is part of my life

My friends/family are always there for me

All my relationships are harmonious and supportive

I am a caring, supportive friend and relative

I am in a wonderful, enduring relationship with someone who really loves me

SELF-CONFIDENCE AND SELF-ESTEEM

Worries

I can't do it

I always mess up

I always say the wrong thing

I don't look good anymore

I'm overweight

Suggested affirmations

I can do it

I am smart, competent and able

I am a confident person; every day my confidence increases to new heights

I have great strength of character and achieve all I set out to do

I inhale confidence, and exhale fear

I trust my intuition and am willing to listen to that still, small voice within

I speak naturally and easily with everyone I meet

I accept myself for who I am

I forgive and look after myself

I am growing and changing for the better

OVERWHELM

Worries

I don't know what to do

Everything's mounting up; I can't get it all done.

I don't know where to start

I just can't seem to get started

I can't switch off; there's so much stuff buzzing around inside my head

Suggested affirmations

I believe everything will work out

I trust my inner guidance

The right decisions come easily to me now

It's okay to ask for help

I have all the time I need to accomplish all I need to do

I know one task at a time is enough

I accomplish everything that needs to get done

I release the need for perfection

I can do anything I put my mind to

I'm calm and relaxed in all situations

POTENTIAL DISASTERS

Worry: *I might be involved in a car crash on the way to work.*
Affirmation: *I have a safe and easy journey to work*

Worry: *My credit cards might be stolen while I'm doing the grocery shopping*
Affirmation: *My credit cards are safe and secure in my bag*

Worry: *I might get mugged on the way home*
Affirmation: *I arrive home safe and sound*

A FEW FINAL THOUGHTS

If you're not noticing any positive change in how you think and feel after using your chosen affirmations and visualisation for a few weeks, consider changing the content, particularly if you feel they're not resonating with you. Before you do this, however, make sure you really have been repeating your affirmations and visualisation night and morning, and as often as you can in-between.

It's also possible to get into a rut with affirmations and start saying them like an automaton without any real feeling or enthusiasm. Do your best to avoid this tendency, because it will be self-defeating. If you find you're not enthusing about your affirmations, change them to something you find more inspiring.

People sometimes ask: *what's the ideal number of affirmations*? There's no simple answer to this question, as it depends very much on you as an individual and what you want to accomplish. What I would say is that it's important to give yourself fully to each of your affirmations, which means putting your heart and soul into them, using an appropriate tone of voice and suitable visualisation, as well as feeling the feeling associated with the affirmation. This can take several minutes, if not longer, so I would recommend going for less rather than more affirmations. Once you've accomplished what you want in one area of your life, you can always move onto another area.